SCHINDLER
EDUCATION CENTER

**University of
NorthernIowa**

Sixth Edition · Revised Print

*Defining the Relationship*

Student Teacher and Cooperating Teacher Handbook

**Kendall Hunt**
publishing company

Cover image provided by University of Northern Iowa

**Kendall Hunt**
publishing company
www.kendallhunt.com
*Send all inquiries to:*
4050 Westmark Drive
Dubuque, IA 52004-1840

Copyright © 1999, 2004, 2005, 2007, 2010, 2014 by University of Northern Iowa
Revised Printing: 2015

ISBN 978-1-4652-7407-6

Printed in the United States of America

# *Defining the Relationship*

The faculty of the Department of Teaching, a department in the College of Education at the University of Northern Iowa, prepared this student teaching handbook. ***Defining the Relationship*** is intended to serve as a guide for our student teachers, their respective cooperating teachers, and the administrators who assist them during the student teaching experience. *In the event you need to contact the Department of Teaching regarding any student teaching matter, please call 319-273-2806 or 273-2202.*

## MISSION STATEMENT
Providing exemplary supervision in diverse environments
to develop collaborative professional educators.

*(NOTE: **Defining the Relationship** is an interactive handbook. Cooperating teachers and student teachers have permission to copy specific working pages, i.e., assessment instruments, observation pages, lesson planning pages, etc., found in this handbook).*

The University of Northern Iowa is an equal opportunity employer and educator with comprehensive plans for affirmative action.

# Contents

**Observation and Evaluation of Student Teachers – 35**

**Frequently Asked Questions (FAQ's) and Forms – 101**

# General Information

**"Integrity is doing the right thing, even if nobody is watching."**
—*Wayne N. Outten*

# A. Introduction

This handbook has been developed to assist student teachers and cooperating teachers who are involved with the student teaching program at the University of Northern Iowa. While the UNI teacher education program is all-encompassing, one underlying theme is that our prospective teachers will be **reflective teachers** who will demonstrate: **knowledge** in specific disciplines, people, and cultures; **human relations skills** for working with all people regardless of race, religion, gender, or special needs; and **professionalism** through ethical conduct, confidentiality for both students and colleagues, and professional relationships by participating in professional activities.

## Student Teaching is the Capstone

The most valuable experience that can be offered to prospective teachers is the opportunity to work alongside an effective classroom teacher. In so doing, the student teacher gains insight into the teaching/learning process as the cooperating teacher co-plans, co-teaches, and mentors these student teachers. While students at the University of Northern Iowa have been given many opportunities to develop and refine their teaching skills through varied clinical settings (many spending over 100 hours in the PreK-12 classroom), the capstone of these experiences is their semester of student teaching.

# B. Definition of Terms

## Student Teacher

Student teachers are university students who are given the opportunity to experience the full role and meaning of teaching in a school setting. Student teachers share with cooperating teachers the instructional responsibilities of a classroom. They work with colleagues, parents, and administrators in becoming teachers. Student teachers learn and practice the skillful art of teaching, under the guidance of cooperating teachers and supervision from the university coordinator/supervisor.

## Cooperating Teacher

Cooperating teachers are responsible for the direct supervision of teacher education students assigned to them. They provide appropriate professional experiences for their student teachers and help gather objective data on their teaching effectiveness. Cooperating teachers share their expertise in teaching as they guide the student teaching experience. The cooperating teachers and university coordinators or supervisors are members of a team that facilitate professional laboratory experiences for the student teachers.

## University Coordinators of Student Teaching

University coordinators of student teaching are faculty members of the University of Northern Iowa. They spend much of their time in school settings working with teacher education students. They share, with cooperating teachers, the responsibility for the professional growth of student teachers. Much of the university coordinator's time is devoted to working collaboratively with school personnel in designing and implementing the most appropriate and effective experiences for each student teacher. Like campus-based faculty members, university coordinators are also actively involved in research, writing, and service activities, which may involve cooperating teachers and their respective school districts.

## C. Student Teacher Relationships Diagram

It is often said, "It takes a village to raise a child." Student teachers come in contact with many different people, all of whom contribute to their overall education and success as a teacher. These people include:

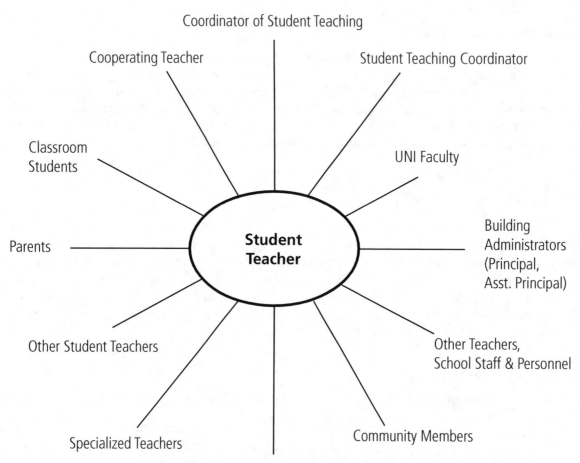

# D. University of Northern Iowa Student Teaching Centers

Student teachers from the University of Northern Iowa fulfill their student teaching requirement in one of the faculty staffed teacher education centers located throughout the state of Iowa, as well as an out-of-state center in Omaha. In addition, we offer out-of-state and international student teaching placements.

Faculty from the various student teaching centers contribute to program improvement through the *Elementary and Secondary Teacher Education Senates.*

## Out-of-State/International Center

# E. Purposes of Student Teaching

The student teaching program at the University of Northern Iowa places priority on developing student teachers' abilities to become reflective, collaborative, and effective practitioners. As a required capstone experience for teacher education students, the program provides a time for learning, experimentation, critical analysis, reflections, and practice. Elements of the teacher/mentor-student/apprentice concept and the inquiry-oriented approach are combined in co-teaching to provide a supportive transition from apprentice to lead teacher. The faculty of the Department of Teaching and the Office of Student Field Experiences developed this statement of goals, which specifies the qualities it seeks to promote in student teachers. Specifically, the program strives to prepare teachers who are:

1. Ready to assume the roles and responsibilities of a beginning teacher.

2. Knowledgeable about effective professional practices and their development.

3. Knowledgeable of ways to modify curriculum, methods, and teacher behaviors that will improve instruction.

4. Capable of demonstrating various styles/models of teaching.

5. Capable of demonstrating working collaboratively with other educators in situations such as co-teaching or professional learning communities.

6. Knowledgeable and skilled in discipline and classroom management procedures.

7. Reflective about ethical consequences of teaching/professional practices.

8. Knowledgeable of the social/democratic/political context of teaching.

9. Knowledgeable of the use of technology to support student learning and professional decision making.

# F. Program Overview

The student teaching program is organized into five curricular components. They are:

1. teaching,
2. supervisory conferences,
3. reflective journal writing/assignments,
4. seminars, and
5. a summative performance assessment.

A brief overview of each component follows.

## Teaching

The teaching experience may take place in a public, private, or accredited school. While each student gradually assumes full responsibility for the instructional program, the central element of the teaching component is the time when the student teacher is allowed to teach on a full-time basis under supervision.

### Co-teaching in Student Teaching

Co-teaching occurs between the student teacher and the cooperating teaching. In co-teaching, two teachers work together to plan, organize, deliver and assess instruction for the students in the assigned class(es).

## Supervisory Conferences

Two- or three-way conferences provide important learning opportunities for the student teacher as well as the cooperating teacher and university coordinator or supervisor. Supervisory conferences may precede and/or follow formal observations by the cooperating teacher and university coordinator or supervisor.

## Reflective Journal Writing/Assignments

The reflective journal is a written dialogue that provides communication between the student teacher and the university coordinator/supervisor. The student teacher initiates the entries and maintains them regularly. At times, in place of journaling, the student teacher may have a written assignment related to their experience.

## Seminars

Seminars are planned and facilitated, in part, by the university coordinator in each center. Seminars are linked to the student teachers' experiences in the classroom.

## Educational Teacher Performance Assessment (edTPA)

The edTPA is an exhibit of teaching performance providing authentic evidence of a candidate's ability to impact student learning through the design and implementation of standards-based instruction. It consists of a written context for the learning, a written explanation of the planning of the learning sequence, a video selection of the learning sequence, and a written analysis of student work (assessment section). Students assess and analyze student learning, and reflect on the teaching and learning process through this work.

# G. The Legal Status of the Student Teacher

The following excerpts from Chapters 262, 272, and 670 of the Code of Iowa describe the legal status of the student teacher.

**Section 262.30 . . . CONTRACTS FOR TRAINING TEACHERS** provides:

The board of directors of any school district in the state of Iowa may enter into contract with the state board of regents for furnishing instruction to pupils of such school district, and for training teachers for the schools of the state in such particular lines of demonstration and instruction as are deemed necessary for the efficiency of the University of Northern Iowa . . . as training schools for teachers.

**Section 272.27 . . . STUDENT TEACHING** provides:

If the rules adopted by the board of educational examiners for issuance of any type or class of license require an applicant to complete work in student teaching, an accredited college or university located within the state of Iowa and states conterminous with Iowa may offer a program or programs of teacher education approved by the director of the department of education or the appropriate authority in states conterminous with Iowa by entering into a written contract with any accredited school district or private school, under terms and conditions as agreed upon by the contracting parties. Students actually teaching in a school district under the terms of such a contract are entitled to the same protection, under section 670.8, as is afforded by that section to officers and employees of the school district, during the time they are so assigned.

**Section 670.8 . . . Officers and employees defended**.

The governing body shall defend its officers and employees, whether elected or appointed and shall save harmless and indemnify the officers and employees against any tort claim or demand, whether groundless or otherwise, arising out of an alleged act or omission occurring within the scope of their employment or duties. However, the duty to save harmless and indemnify does not apply to awards for punitive damages. The exception for punitive damages does not prohibit a governing body from purchasing insurance to protect its officers and employees from punitive damages. The duty to save harmless and indemnify does not apply and the municipality is entitled to restitution by an officer or employee if, in an action commenced by the municipality against the officer or employee, it is determined that the conduct of the officer or employee upon which the tort claim or demand was based constituted a willful and wanton act or omission. Any independent or autonomous board or commission of a municipality having authority to disburse funds for a particular municipal function without approval of the governing body shall similarly defend, save harmless and indemnify its officers and employees against tort claims or demands.

The duties to defend and to save harmless and indemnify shall apply whether or not the municipality is a party to the action and shall include but not be limited to cases arising under title 42 United States Code section 1983.

In the event the officer or employee fails to cooperate in the defense against the claim or demand, the municipality shall have a right of indemnification against that officer or employee.

## References

State Code of Iowa (1997). *Contracts for Training Teachers*, Vol. II – Chap. 262, p. 2267.
State Code of Iowa (1997). *Student Teaching*, Vol. II – Chap. 272, p. 2313.
State Code of Iowa (1997). *Officers and Employees Defended*, Vol. II – Chap. 670, p. 5763.

# H. Iowa Code of Professional Conduct and Ethics

(complete text at: http://www.boee.iowa.gov/doc/ethHndot.pdf)

*282—25.3(272)* Standards of professional conduct and ethics. Violation of federal, state, or local laws in the fulfillment of professional obligations constitutes unprofessional and unethical conduct which can result in disciplinary action by the board.

25.3(1) Standard I—conviction of crimes, sexual or other immoral conduct with or toward a student, and child and dependent adult abuse. (fraud, criminal convictions, sexual abuse, student abuse, and sexual exploitation)

25.3(2) Standard II—alcohol or drug abuse.

25.3(3) Standard III—misrepresentation, falsification of information. (applications, compliance reports, official inquiries or investigations, license renewal, student evaluations or test information)

25.3(4) Standard IV—misuse of public funds and property. (educational funds, request for funds, school-related funds, use of time and funds)

25.3(5) Standard V—violations of contractual obligations. (multiple contracts, teaching in non-licensed area, breaking contracts)

25.3(6) Standard VI—unethical practice toward other members of the profession, parents, students, and the community. (discriminating acts, accepting gifts, closed to student views, disclosing confidential information, exposing students to unnecessary risks or embarrassment, soliciting for personal gain, etc.)

25.3(7) Standard VII—compliance with state law governing student loan obligations and child support obligations. (student loans, child support )

25.3(8) Standard VIII—incompetence. (willfully/repeatedly failing to conform to standards)


# I. University Policies Related to Personal Conduct

Student teachers are subject to provisions of the Student Disciplinary Code and other University of Northern Iowa policies and procedures governing personal conduct. Examples include policies regarding use of computers, sexual assault, academic ethics, drugs, alcohol, discrimination, harassment, etc. These policies may be accessed at http://www.uni.edu/vpess/handbook.html.

# Responsibilities of Student Teachers

**Note**: Co-Teaching Models & Professional Learning Communities are found in the *Responsibilities of School and University Personnel Section* and need to be read and understood by each student teacher.

**"Tell me and I forget. Teach me and I remember. *Involve me* and I learn."**
—*Benjamin Franklin*

**"Differentiation just asks of us what we ask of our students, flexible thinking, intellectual risk taking, problem solving,---and a deeping sense of humanity."**
—*Carol Tomilinson*

# A. What it Means to Be a Reflective Teacher

In 1933, John Dewey made an important distinction in conceptualizing teachers' practices when he identified routine and reflective action. He defined routine action as teaching acts characterized by authority, impulse, and tradition. Persons who teach from this perspective uncritically accept the defined practices of schools and set about to find the most efficient and effective way to carry out these practices. They overlook the possibility that other, if not more desirable, options exist. For example, day-to-day school practices (e.g., the goals, problems, and methods of solving problems) are dealt with routinely. To the extent that everyday practices continue in prescribed ways without major interruption, schooling practices are typically viewed as non-problematic, that is, not warranting examination or change.

Conversely, Dewey defines reflective action ". . . as behavior which involves active, persistent, and careful consideration of any belief or practice in light of the grounds that support it and the further consequences to which it leads" (Grant and Zeichner, 1984). Reflective action involves meeting and responding to problems. Persons who teach from this perspective actively analyze their teaching practices and the educational, social, democratic, and political contexts in which their teaching is embedded. For example, traditional planning practices are examined, and alternative planning methods are explored.

Dewey refers to three attitudes as prerequisite to reflective action. They are: 1) **open-mindedness**, 2) **responsibility**, and 3) **wholeheartedness**.

Dewey's concept of **open-mindedness** refers to an active desire to consider more than one perspective, to give full attention to alternate possibilities, and to recognize the possibility of error, even in the beliefs that are dearest to us. To be open-minded implies that alternate solutions to existing practices can and probably should be explored. Reflective teaching means that teachers hold attitudes that are characterized by open-mindedness about the content, methods, and procedures used in the classroom and will critically analyze traditional practices.

An attitude of **responsibility**, according to Dewey, involves thorough consideration of the consequences that result from their teaching action. Responsibility requires teachers to ask themselves why they are doing what they are doing in the classroom. Teachers have an obligation to consider the consequences of their decisions as they relate to the lives of the students they teach.

The third and final attitude, **wholeheartedness**, implies that open-mindedness and responsibility are central to the lives of reflective teachers who vigorously seek out and assume responsibility for the education of their students. An attitude of wholeheartedness requires a dedicated and committed approach to teaching all students, not just a few, and impels the teacher to learn about the uniqueness of each student so that optimal educational experiences can be supplied.

# B. Student Teaching Pledge

As a student teacher at the University of Northern Iowa, I pledge that I shall:

❏ Develop knowledge of human development, learning, and sociocultural factors as the essential basis for pedagogical decision-making.

❏ Develop skills of observation, reflection, decision-making, and leadership.

❏ Develop those literacy, numeracy, critical, and creative thinking abilities, and the ethical values associated with the concept of an educated person.

❏ Gain knowledge of, and the ability to use, effective teaching skills and techniques, effective communication skills, and team-teaching (co-teaching) proficiency.

❏ Develop a collaborative relationship with my cooperating teacher(s) and school personnel in order to share responsibility for a group of students and work collaboratively to add instructional value for all students (co-teaching).

❏ Develop the ability to transform content knowledge into educational activities that engage all students and advance their learning.

❏ Demonstrate a commitment to professional development and growth, actively participating in the professional development opportunities at my school.

❏ Demonstrate a growing sense of professional responsibility to the profession and those it serves.

❏ Demonstrate an awareness and understanding of the social and moral responsibility that underlies the practice of the profession and a commitment to the Iowa Code of Professional Conduct and Ethics.

❏ Demonstrate the values, commitments and professional ethics in my professional practice such as caring, fairness, honesty, responsibility, and social justice. As such, during student teaching, I will:

  • Practice patience and flexibility as I learn the art of teaching from my cooperating teacher and other professional colleagues.

  • Ask questions and seek help when needed.

  • Maintain a professional appearance.

  • Be prepared and punctual for class/appointments.

  • Respond positively to constructive criticism as I realize I am here to learn.

  • Demonstrate compliance with laws/regulations/policies/standards.

  • Demonstrate respect for the beliefs of others and cultural differences.

In this way, I can become a teacher who is a responsible, reflective and effective decision-maker in a global society.

# C. Statement of Commitment & Acknowledgement of Consequences

I have read the Student Teaching Pledge found in the UNI Student Teaching Handbook and the Iowa Code of Professional Conduct and Ethics (complete text found at: http://www.boee.iowa.gov/doc/ethHndot.pdf). I believe that adhering to all the tenets in these documents are critical for my success in student teaching. I am committed to growing throughout my student teaching experience and demonstrating excellence in these tenets.

I understand I will transition into the lead teacher in the classroom through a series of gradual steps, from a short period of observation, to providing support to my cooperating teacher by helping individual students, taking small groups of students for instruction, co-planning with my cooperating teacher, team teaching with my cooperating teacher, serving as a lead teacher for a class/subject area, and gradually adding a class/subject area until I am leading classes/subject areas for the entire day.

I understand that my Student Teaching Coordinator(s) and my Cooperating Teacher(s) or other professional colleagues will provide constructive criticism of my performance to help me grow as a teacher. I will respond positively to this constructive criticism and use it in my next teaching sequences.

## Acknowledgement of Consequences

I also understand that student teaching is my priority. I understand my cooperating teacher/student teaching coordinator will identify my areas of strength and weaknesses and will help me work on each. I understand if I continue to struggle or do not work on identified areas of weakness, I will receive a Notice of Concern (NOC). I know I should look to the NOC as an opportunity to focus on improvement. In most cases, student teachers focus and demonstrate improvement and the NOC is resolved. Should I not improve, I realize there will be consequences. (More on Professional Competencies and NOC can be found at www.uni.edu/teachered/professional-competencies.)

If at any time I am removed from my student teaching placement, at the request of the school or the student teaching coordinator, or I fail to show adequate ratings on the student teaching final evaluation, I will receive No Credit (NC) for this placement. I understand I will then have to make a written application for the next student teaching placement and will have to complete and pay for an additional eight weeks of student teaching placement. Please be advised, if a student teacher receives No Credit from **two** student teaching placements s/he cannot be recommended for teacher licensure by the University of Northern Iowa. If I withdraw from student teaching, I understand I will receive an NOC documenting my withdrawal and explaining the next steps should I want to obtain my teaching certificate in the future.

_____    _____
UNI Student ID             Printed Name


_____    _____
Date                       Signature

# D. Expectations for Student Teaching

The student teaching program is organized into five curricular components. They are:

1. teaching,
2. supervisory conferences,
3. reflective journal writing,
4. seminars, and
5. a summative performance assessment.

A brief overview of each component follows.

## Teaching

The teaching experience may take place in a public, private, or accredited school. While each student gradually assumes full responsibility for the instructional program, the central element of the teaching component is the time when the student teacher is allowed to teach on a full-time basis under supervision.

### Co-teaching in Student Teaching

Co-teaching occurs between the student teacher and the cooperating teacher. In co-teaching, two teachers work together to plan, organize, deliver, and assess instruction for the students in the assigned class(es). In the beginning the cooperating teacher is the lead teacher, modeling the planning process, the instruction, and the assessment and the student teacher plays the supporting role, helping individual students, monitoring learning, and providing small group instruction. The student teacher is expected to gradually transition into the lead teacher role, assuming responsibility for classroom management, planning and teaching lessons within the curriculum of the classroom, using a variety of teaching strategies, and providing for the individual needs of pupils in both planning and evaluation. Student teachers are to **assume full responsibility in the classroom for a minimal length of two weeks** during an eight-week placement, with the cooperating teacher playing a supporting role. It is important to be able to evaluate the student teacher's ability to be in charge of the entire classroom experience.

## Supervisory Conferences

Two- or three-way conferences provide important learning opportunities for the student teacher as well as the cooperating teacher and university coordinator or supervisor. Supervisory conferences may precede and/ or follow formal observations by the cooperating teacher and university coordinator or supervisor.

During conferences, university coordinators/supervisors have an opportunity to raise issues that were introduced in seminars, as well as provide feedback about specific teaching practices. When making formal observations, supervisors prepare narrative notes that will be shared and discussed with the student teacher for the purpose of promoting growth. Student teachers are expected to respond positively to this constructive feedback and utilize this feedback to improve their lessons, pedagogy, management, or dispostions.

## Reflective Journal Writing

The reflective journal is a written dialogue that provides communication between the student teacher and the university coordinator/supervisor. The student teacher initiates the entries and maintains them regularly. The entries provide a means for critically analyzing classroom activities, intellectual and emotional reflections and attitudes, as well as questions concerning teaching, learning procedures, and practices. This reflective record may become a source of evaluation for past performances and a projection for change, innovation, and practice for the future.

## Seminars

Seminars are planned and facilitated, in part, by the university coordinator in each center. Seminars are linked to the student teachers' experiences in the classroom. They are designed to broaden the students' knowledge of teaching by encouraging reflection on practice through the consideration of educational alternatives and their consequences.

## Educational Teacher Performance Assessment (edTPA)

The edTPA is an exhibit of teaching performance providing authentic evidence of a candidate's ability to impact student learning through the design and implementation of standards-based instruction. It consists of a written context for the learning, a written explanation of the planning of the learning sequence, a video selection of the learning sequence, and a written analysis of student work (assessment section). Students assess and analyze student learning, and reflect on the teaching and learning process through this work.

Guided by the Teacher Performance Assessment Rubrics, the teacher candidate will be expected to document his or her ability to:

1. Use information about the learning/teaching context and student individual differences to set learning goals, plan instruction, and assess learning.
2. Set significant, challenging, varied, and appropriate learning goals.
3. Use multiple assessment modes and approaches aligned with the learning goals to assess student learning before, during, and after instruction.
4. Design instruction for specific learning goals, student characteristics and needs, and learning contexts.
5. Use ongoing analysis of student learning to make instructional decisions.
6. Use assessment data (student work) to profile student learning and communicate information about student progress and achievement.
7. Analyze the relationship between his or her instruction and student learning in order to improve teaching practice.

The Teacher Performance Assessment is one of multiple measures, along with classroom observations, midterm and final student teaching evaluations to assess teaching performance relative to national and state teaching standards.. The finished product can provide an important artifact that displays evidence consistent with requirements for permanent teaching licensure.

Trained professors and practicing teachers will score the Teacher Performance Assessment and provide feedback to the student teachers. A group of the Teacher Performance Assessments may also be scored nationally.

# E. Responsibilities of the Student Teacher

The student teaching program at the University of Northern Iowa places priority on developing student teachers' abilities to become reflective practitioners. As a required field experience for teacher education students, the program provides a time for learning, experimentation, critical analysis, co-teaching, and practice. In so doing, the student teacher will have certain responsibilities ascribed to them. They will:

1. Bring to the teaching experience adequate knowledge in the areas of basic subject matter, human growth and development, and teaching strategies and procedures.

2. Display a highly professional attitude with respect to confidential information about children and youth, and with respect to relationships and practices with colleagues and the respective educational systems.

3. Abide by patterns of conduct expected of professional personnel.

4. Strive to exemplify the attitudes and actions of a teacher rather than those of a student.

5. Demonstrate responsibility in accepting and completing assigned tasks.

6. Place duties and responsibilities ahead of personal desires.

7. Adhere to the Code of Ethics of the Education Profession.

8. Display enthusiasm and interest in all phases of the teaching experience.

9. Plan all work and submit plans to the cooperating teacher and the university coordinator/supervisor (if required) prior to teaching a lesson. Include, when necessary, safety rules for the pupils to follow.

10. Attempt a variety of teaching techniques (discovery, problem solving, lecture, simulations, discussion, independent learning, games, demonstrations, co-teaching, and co-planning, etc.) in an effort to discover and develop a personal style of teaching. If needed, set short-term goals for improvement of communication skills (voice quality and projection, non-verbal skills, use of media, opening motivators and closure, etc.).

11. Experience the use of technology and varied media in the instructional process. Prepare bulletin boards and displays to accompany and enhance on-going classroom work.

12. Assume responsibilities in identifying student needs. If necessary, provide alternative methods for non-readers or other special-needs children so they may obtain the required information from the printed page.

13. Analyze classroom interaction in order to determine the degree of participation by the various members of the class and alter such interaction if deemed appropriate.

14. Design varied tests and/or evaluation procedures. Then select, use, and interpret objective data, records, and lesson designs to facilitate in understanding and guiding pupil growth. Follow up with appropriate remedial or "challenge" lessons.

15. Participate in one or more extra-curricular activities, including parent-teacher conferences. And, if available, share in the preparation of formal pupil progress reports to parents.

16. Interact with pupils in informal situations (playgrounds, corridors, school functions, library, study halls, lunch room, etc.).

17. Accept constructive feedback and engage in regular self-appraisal.

18. Read the school policy manual to become familiar with essential information in order to comply with all school system and building regulations, including the school calendar, which regularly employed teachers are expected to observe.

19. Assume supervisory responsibilities (playground, corridors, lunchrooms, buses, school events, etc.) with the cooperating teacher, but not in lieu of the cooperating teacher.

20. Interact with non-teaching personnel (custodians, secretaries, nurses, cooks, etc.) and discover how all must relate effectively within the school setting.

21. Develop an understanding of the role of administrators, teachers, lay people, support staff, and the Board of Education in determining school policies and in decision making.

22. Observe a variety of classes (unique programs, exemplary teachers, varied levels, etc.). Check with the cooperating teacher and/or the building principal as to who might be the best teachers to observe.

23. Contact the cooperating teacher and university coordinator/supervisor when ill and turn in the appropriate form to the university coordinator.

24. Complete reflective journals or assignments as directed by the university coordinator.

25. Student teachers with disabilities are encouraged to address any special needs or special accommodations with their cooperating teacher at the beginning of their placement or as soon as they become aware of their needs. Those seeking accommodations based on a disability should contact Student Disability Services (SDS) (phone 319-273-2677, for deaf or hard of hearing, use Relay 711). SDS is located on the top floor of the Student Health Center, Room 103. SDS will collaborate with the student and the Teacher Education Program to determine reasonable

# F. Attendance Requirements for Student Teachers

Students are expected to follow the district's schedule of the teachers' school day (including IEP meetings, professional development activities, content-related meetings, parent-teacher conferences, etc.). Student teachers will follow the district's calendar for all holidays, vacations, and make up days during the placement period.

Excessive absence (excused or unexcused) from duty may result in the termination of the student teacher assignment. The length of the student teaching period shall be a factor in the decision to terminate. Reasons for absences may include illness, emergency situations, interviews, or other appropriate professional reasons.

Student teachers who are registered for twelve (12) hours of credit, fulfilling the student teaching requirement in the same cooperating center, and who are absent from student teaching a total of six (6) or more instructional days may be withdrawn from their student teaching assignment. A "NC" (no credit) will be recorded if the student is withdrawn after the last day to drop without penalty.

The decision to terminate a student teaching assignment due to absence from duty is the responsibility of the university coordinator of student teaching acting in consort with the cooperating teacher, building principal, supervisor, and the Coordinator of Student Teaching. The student teacher, however, may be permitted to make up the days missed by extending the student teaching period in extentuating circumstances. Consideration should be given to this option instead of termination, provided the performance level of the student teacher indicates potential for completion of the experience with a "competent" or higher evaluation. In the event termination from student teaching is determined to be the best course of action, the student teacher shall have avenues for appeal and due process, as accorded by university policy.

# G. Guidelines in the Absence of the Cooperating Teacher

## Policy Statement

A student teacher from the University of Northern Iowa fulfilling the student teaching requirement shall not be used as a substitute teacher for a cooperating teacher or any other teacher. The rationale for this policy is that the student is not licensed and therefore is prevented by the Code of Iowa to have the authority to control student conduct in unsupervised situations. This policy also applies to other duties, e.g., hall duty, lunchroom duty, bus duty, etc. Student teachers should assist in these responsibilities, but not in lieu of the cooperating teacher.

## Guidelines

If the absence of the cooperating teacher occurs at a later time in the experience, the student teacher could assume more responsibility for teaching, but under the supervision of a licensed substitute teacher. Building principals are legally responsible for the welfare and supervision of all classrooms in their charge in the absence of the cooperating teacher.

# H. Absences from Student Teaching

Information on any unplanned absences from student teaching should be conveyed to your cooperating teacher and university coordinator with a phone call, text, and/or email. The specific reasons for the absence need to be explained and a contingency plan should be described. If the absence is planned, you must complete this form and obtain all needed signatures prior to the planned absence.

## Planned Absence Approval Form

_____

Name of Student Teacher

Today's date _____ Date(s) of leave _____

_____ _____ a.m. _____ p.m. _____ both

**Reason for absence:**

_____

_____

**Contingency Plan:** *(Specify who will assume your duties and/or where the directions for these duties can be found. If this were unexpected and you were to teach, did you provide substitute lesson plans?)*

_____

_____

_____

Signed. _____
(Student Teacher)

Signed. _____
(Cooperating Teacher)

**Cooperating Teacher please check one:**

_____ Approved      _____ Not Approved

# I. Working While Student Teaching

1. Employment during student teaching is discouraged. Student teaching is considered a full-time responsibility. If a student teacher is employed prior to student teaching, he/she should discontinue that employment or get the number of hours pared back so as not to have employment interfere with student teaching. The student teaching coordinator, along with input from the cooperating teacher, has the right to request a student teacher to alter a work schedule if they believe it is interfering with the student teacher's classroom performance. Check with your coordinator about any site-specific requirements regarding employment.

2. Student teachers wishing to coach may volunteer by letting the coordinator know of their desire to coach. The university supervisor has the right to terminate or alter a student teacher's coaching experience if s/he believes it is interfering with the student teacher's classroom performance. Check with your coordinator about any site-specific requirements regarding coaching during student teaching.

## References Listed

Apple, M. & N. King. 1977. *What Do Schools Teach?* Curriculum Inquiry, Vol. 6, pp. 341–357.

Chapman, C. and Hyatt, C.H. 2011. *Critical Conversations in Co-Teaching*. Bloomington, Indiana: Solution Tree Press.

Dewey, J. 1933. *How We Think: A Restatement of the Relation of Reflective Thinking to the Educative Teaching*. Chicago: Henry Regnery.

DuFour, R. 2004. *Schools as Learning Communities*. Educational Leadership. Vol. 61. No. 8, pp. 6–11. *What is a Professional Learning Community*? Retrieved March 17, 2014 from: http://www.ascd.org/publications/educational-leadership/may04/vol61/num08/What-Is-a-Professional-Learning-Community%C2%A2.aspx

Gothe. K. 2013. *Dynamics of the Relationship Between Student Teachers and Master Teachers within the Co-Teaching Model*. (Master of Arts Thesis). School of Education. Biola University, La Mirada, Ca. Retrieved from ERIC Database (ED542506). 104 pp.

Grant, C.A. & K.M. Zeichner. 1985. *The Teacher*. In C.A. Grant's (ed.) Preparing for Reflective Teaching. Boston: Allyn and Bacon, Inc., pp. 1–18.

Professional Learning Communities: Professional Development Strategies That Improve Instruction. Annenberg Institute for School Reform. Retrieved March 17, 2014 from http://annenberginstitute.org/pdf/proflearning.pdf

Zeichner, K. 1981. *Reflective Teaching and Field-based Experiences in Teacher Education*. Interchange. Vol. 12, pp. 1–22.

# Responsibilities of School and University Personnel

A. Responsibilities of the Cooperating Teacher

B. Co-Teaching Models

C. Professional Learning Communities (PLCs)

D. Suggested Timeline for Working with Student Teachers

E. Lesson Planning with the Student Teacher

F. Focus Questions for Student Teacher's Lesson Plans

G. Responsibilities of the University Coordinator/Supervisor

H. Suggested Responsibilities of Building Administrators

"Supervision can be a place where a living profession breathes and learns."
—*Robin Hawkins and Peter Shohet*

"Supervison is an opportunity to bring someone back to their own mind,
to show them how good they can be."
—*Nancy Kline*

# A. Responsibililites of the Cooperating Teacher

The role of the cooperating teacher cannot be taken too lightly. The cooperating teacher is the initial mentor of the student teacher during the student teaching experience. Therefore, the cooperating teacher is encouraged to:

1. Prepare their pupils for the arrival of the student teacher, emphasizing the fact that this will be a teaching team with the student teacher having an authoritative position.

2. Provide a desk, file drawer space, and a place for coats and belongings.

3. Provide the student teacher with seating charts or some means for the student teacher to become familiar with the names of the students they will be working with.

4. Share information about the cultural background of their students, as well as helpful information about each student.

5. Describe the cultural make-up of the school and the economic and social conditions of the neighborhood.

6. Discuss with the student teacher the expected behaviors as appropriate with their respective classrooms, school buildings, and in conjunction with the responsibilities as described in the previous section for the student teacher.

7. Clarify the philosophy and goals of teaching with the student teacher. Explain how classroom management is governed according to this philosophy. Orient the student teacher to your classroom management system.

8. Set up definite procedures for conferencing and co-planning to mentor the student teacher in the lesson planning process. This ensures the student teacher understands the type of lesson plan you expect.

9. Assist the student teacher during the first full week by providing an observation guide that will help make this time valuable.

10. Work within the co-teaching models to develop a tentative short-range and long-range plan for the student teacher to assume lead classroom responsibilities.

11. Allow the student teacher to first work with individual students and small groups and gradually assume the responsibility for the entire class. Provide opportunities for co-teaching to model best practice. (In an eight-week placement, it is suggested that the lead responsibility for teaching the entire class be a two-week minimum.)

12. Systematically observe, and analyze the performance of the student teacher and provide substantive feedback to the student teacher.

13. Encourage the student teacher to observe ways to enrich the curriculum by bringing outside materials from the curriculum laboratory or other sources into the classroom.

14. Acquaint the student teacher with audiovisual equipment in the school, the procedures for securing the same, and give the necessary help to ensure effective use. Also acquaint the student teacher about the use and access to AEA resources.

15. Discuss hall procedures, lunchroom procedures, recess procedures, bus procedures, etc., so the student teacher may act responsibly when assisting the cooperating teacher with these duties.

16. Help establish good rapport between the student teacher and other school personnel.

17. Orient the student teacher to the school building, regulations, use of machines, materials, and supplies.

18. Orient the student teacher as to the school's professional expectations.

## Teacher Performance Assessment Responsibilities (edTPA)

Cooperating teachers are encouraged to provide direction and assistance with the following:

1. Contextual Factors: Direct students to resources for information such as free and reduced lunch percentages, ethnicity reports, grade level test data, student learning levels, and other relevant data.

2. Help students find the lists of students, who do not agree to be video-taped for the edTPA learning segments and allow these students to be seated outside the camera view. (These learning segments may be viewed by the student teacher, cooperating teacher, scoring personnel, or for educational uses only.)

3. Provide the opportunity to teach student-centered lessons. These may be provided by the cooperating teacher, adapted by student teacher, or lessons the student teacher creates.

4. Check the appropriateness of the assessment for the grade level and content area.

# B.  Co-Teaching Models

Co-teaching as well as independent teaching, should be a part of each student teaching placement. There are many models of co-teaching. There is no order in which these models should be implemented in the student teaching placement, nor will all necessarily be used. No matter which co-teaching model is utilized, the planning process needs to occur together with the cooperating teacher and the student teacher, allowing the student teacher to learn how lessons are developed. In a co-teaching relationship, not only does the master cooperating teacher explain and demonstrate his/her craft, s/he nurtures the novice student teacher in learning the craft of teaching. Initially the cooperating teacher will be in the lead role and the student teacher will be in the supporting role. The student teacher will gradually take on the lead role in a class and build up until s/he is independently teaching for a minimum of two weeks in an eight-week placement. During this time, the cooperating teacher plays a supportive role for the student teacher.

❑ **One Teach, One Observe** – One teacher has the primary instructional responsibility (lead teacher) while the other gathers specific information on students or the teacher (supporting teacher). The focus is on observation – where and how the teacher is implementing the instruction and observing specific behaviors. It is anticipated that the student teacher would start in the observation mode and finish his or her student teaching placement in the lead teacher role.

❑ **One Teach, One Assist** – This is much like the one teach, one observe model, but in this model the lead teacher instructs the class, while the supporting teacher assists students with their work, monitors behaviors, corrects assignments, assesses student understanding, and may participate in classroom discussions.

❑ **Station Teaching** – In this model both the cooperating teacher and the student teacher split the lead teacher responsibilities and each one instructs a group of students who rotate through the instructional stations.

❑ **Parallel Teaching** – In this model both the student teacher and the cooperating teacher are a lead teacher to a subset of students. Both are presenting the same materials and using the same teaching strategies, but each as a smaller group of students.

❑ **Team Teaching** – In this model both the cooperating teacher and the student teacher take alternating lead roles. The instructional transitions are seamlessly planned and implemented with both teachers actively involved.

❑ **Supplemental Teaching** – In this model both the cooperating and student teacher are lead teachers, but one works with students at their grade level, while the other works with students who need extra help, re-teaching, or extensions.

# C. Professional Learning Communities (PLCs)

A professional learning community is a group of educational professionals working together to ensure that students' are not just taught, but also learn. They usually meet regularly over a significant period of time. These PLCs often focus on three critical questions: 1) What do we want every student to learn, 2) How will we know they have learned it, and 3) What do we do when a student has difficulty learning?

Paramount in PLCs is the culture of collaboration. Without working together it is difficult to quickly identify students who need additional help, develop a plan to provide this help, and systematically administer the plan and expect students to devote the time needed to master the concepts.

Finally, effective PLCs are data driven, focusing on results. This data is collected to determine the impact of the "implemented interventions" upon students learning. Continual improvement is the goal. Student teachers are expected to participate in a PLC, if one is available.

# D. Suggested Timeline for Working with Student Teachers

The student teaching experience can be broken down into three vital areas: **observation** (One Teach, One Observe), **participation** (One Teach, One Assist; Station Teaching), and **teaching** (Parallel Teaching, Team Teaching, & Supplemental Teaching). The rate at which a student teacher progresses through each stage is an individual matter based on the abilities of the student teacher. Some student teachers, out of necessity, need to work longer in observation and participation than do others. There is no set length of time before a student teacher is "ready" to start lead teaching. The cooperating teacher needs to gather enough data to be able to determine the student teacher's readiness to independently lead his/her own classroom. It is recommended that a minimum of two weeks in an eight-week placement, be spent in the lead teaching phase. However, the cooperating teacher should use her/his professional judgment as to the length of time spent in the co-teaching and independent teaching phase.

**Week One—Observation: One Teach, One Observe**

1. **Purpose**
   a. To understand the particular classroom situation.
   b. To understand the role of the teacher in specific classroom situations.
   c. To develop an awareness of individual qualities of pupils in order to clearly understand the classroom atmosphere.
   d. To have time to learn the student's names and begin to sense their personal learning styles, as well as analyze individual differences.
   e. To co-plan with the cooperating teacher so that the student teacher can understand lesson plan explanations and materials/resouces available.
   f. To give the student teacher time to adjust to the class environment so that as she/he eventually moves into the lead teaching phase, she/he will not upset the learning process.

2. **Observing the teaching process**
   a. To determine the teacher's purpose for the particular lesson.
   b. To observe the motivation process.
   c. To note pupil response and interest in the materials, technology, and media used. This is a great time to have the student teacher collect specific data on students in the classroom to support the learning process.
   d. To visualize the lesson as a part of the overall unit and observe the evidence of planning for this lesson.
   e. To observe the cooperating teacher for relevant modeling.

3. **Observation of all elements that affect the class disposition**
   a. To observe how the transition is made from one subject area to another.
   b. To attempt to analyze techniques and principles that lead to effective classroom management.

### Week Two—Participation: One Teach, One Assist; Station Teaching

1. **Purpose**
   a. To provide a transition between observation and lead teaching.
   b. To provide activities that enhance the observation process, provide a greater understanding of teaching, and allow the student teacher to become more familiar with the student teaching process.

2. **Opportunities for sharing non-teaching materials**
   a. To assist with assembling and preparing materials for a particular lesson.
   b. To assist with non-teaching routines of the school.
   c. To co-plan with the cooperating teacher in preparing a specific lesson plans and/or units. *(See Section B Co-Teaching Models.)*

### Week Three—Participation/Teaching: Station Teaching, Parallel Teaching, Team Teaching & Supplemental Teaching

1. Purpose
   a. To provide a period of cooperative teaching where both the student teacher and cooperating teacher share the "lead teaching" at various times.
   b. To continue to develop lesson plans with the cooperating teacher.
   c. To collect and/or prepare materials to be used in the teaching of a lesson or unit.

### Week Four, Five, Six, and Seven—Co-Teaching evolving into Independent Teaching

1. Purpose
   a. During this time the lead teaching switches to the student teacher the majority of time. The cooperating teacher serves as the supporting teacher until which point the student teacher takes the entire lead teaching all classes.
   b. To provide a time period where the lesson plans are the personal development of the student teacher.
   c. To provide for individual differences through careful selection of materials and procedures to meet varying learning capabilities.
   d. To make the plan work by:
      1. Stimulating interest through questions that require in-depth attention.
      2. Utilizing all opportunities for effective use of visual aids.
      3. Recognizing that teaching must fit within the framework of the prescribed course of study.
      4. Providing for a smooth transition from one activity to another.
      5. Developing flexibility in carrying out plans.
      6. Summarizing the lesson to assure understanding.
   e. To produce an evaluation instrument to measure learning.

### Week Eight—Participation/Observation

1. **Purpose**
   a. To bring closure to the student teaching experience and to allow the cooperating teacher to reclaim the classroom.
   b. To enable the student teacher to observe other notable teachers and/or programs.

# E. Lesson Planning with the Student Teacher

Lesson planning is essential to effective teaching and, therefore, it is important for the cooperating teacher to co-plan with the student teacher. This allows him/her to intimately understand the nuances of lesson planning to meet Iowa core and classroom needs. The cooperating teacher can provide insights into meeting individual needs in the classroom, while at the same time helping the student teacher develop the skills of effective short- and long-term planning. As student teacher progresses through their placement s/he should show the initiative to take the lead in lesson planning. Their plans should be detailed, providing an outline of objectives and activities to guide learning experiences, suggested individualization and assessments. The cooperating teacher must have an opportunity to read and react to the student teacher's lesson plans to be assured that the student teacher demonstrates the essentials of effective planning, and the progress of pupils is not jeopardized. Following are some guidelines for lesson plan development.

## First weeks of student teaching

Normally, student teachers begin teaching from the plans developed by the cooperating teacher. In utilizing these lessons the student teacher can see the connection between careful planning and effective instruction. It is important in these weeks for the cooperating teacher to co-plan with the student teacher to facilitate this process.

Following a conference with the cooperating teacher in which the proposed content, activities, and strategies are discussed, the student teacher independently prepares the lesson plan. The plan is then made available to the cooperating teacher for further suggestions and approval. The cooperating teacher should see lesson plans well in advance so that ample time for alterations is available and a successful learning experience can be anticipated. It is important for the cooperating teacher and student teacher to thoroughly analyze initial lessons so that optimal learning can be ensured.

## Middle weeks of student teaching

As the student teacher assumes more teaching responsibility, the cooperating teacher should continue to:

1.  Discuss proposed content, activities, and strategies;

2.  Review and respond to lesson plans well in advance of instruction; and,

3.  Conference with the student teacher regarding the connection between quality of the lesson plans and success of the lessons.

## Full-time teaching weeks

The detail of lesson plans may decrease slightly as you become convinced of your student teacher's ability to organize and implement effective plans. As you are apt to be absent (yet available) from the classroom during portions of this time period, it is essential that you know exactly what is happening in your classroom.

# F. Focus Questions for Student Teacher's Lesson Plans

1. **Objectives**
   a. Are the objectives specific?
   b. Will their attainment help pupils to help themselves? Help others?
   c. Are the objectives realistic in terms of the needs and abilities of pupils?
   d. Is thinking encouraged at appropriate cognitive levels?

2. **Materials, Technology, Media**
   a. Are the materials clearly identified, available and organized?
   b. Has it been indicated when and how the materials will be used?

3. **Motivation**
   a. Is the lesson engaging?
   b. Is the plan designed to appeal to the students' interests and developmental abilities?
   c. Does the plan help answer the questions "Why?" "So what?" "What's the point?"
   d. How does this lesson relate to previous class work...to future class work?

4. **Methods**
   a. Has a probable time line been established?
   b. Are the methods appropriate to carrying out the stated objectives?
   c. Do they provide, at least in part, for the range of interest and ability in this particular class?
   d. Have sufficient examples been included to demonstrate the idea or procedure?
   e. What choices have students been given in this lesson?
   f. If questions are to be used in the lesson, have leading questions been formulated?
   g. Is enough work planned to keep pupils engaged in productive tasks?
   h. What problems in management might occur? (Identify possible solutions to these instances for the student teacher.)
   i. Where in the lesson are there checks for understanding?

5. **Assignments**
   a. Is the assignment clear and concise?
   b. Do the pupils know what they are to do? Why it is being assigned? How it is to be done?
   c. Has time been allowed to discuss the assignment with the pupils?
   d. Have provisions been made for individual differences?
   e. Have the students been told how to complete any reading that is assigned?
   f. Have the students been told how to study for a form of assessment that might accompany the lesson?

# G. Responsibilities of the University Coordinator/Supervior

The university coordinator is the manager of the regional student teaching center. It is the university coordinator's responsibility, to place and supervise the student teachers in their respective classroom assignments. The university coordinator and/or supervisor:

1.  Informs the cooperating teacher of any university expectations.

2.  Confers with the cooperating teacher about the student teacher placed with them.

3.  Serves as a resource person to the cooperating teacher, student teacher, or the principal.

4.  Informs the cooperating teacher of due dates for any reports, conferences, and evaluations.

5.  Writes a report after each observation, reporting on the strengths and/or weaknesses of the student teacher.

6.  Visits the student teacher, on site, at least every other week as recommended by the university. Circumstances may dictate more frequent visits; however, the length of these visits will depend entirely upon the needs and wishes of the particular student, the cooperating teacher, and the university supervisor.

7.  Extend professional services to the center school systems.

8.  Provides the necessary orientation for student teachers concerning their responsibilities.

9.  Counsels with individual student teachers concerning personal and professional problems.

# H. Suggested Responsibilities of Building Administrators

The building administrator is the administrator for a given building or buildings. She/he is responsible for what happens in their respective building(s). She/he works directly with the teachers and staff in their respective building(s). A student teacher should be considered as another teacher in their building(s) and should be expected to function in a similar capacity. Regarding student teachers, the building administrator is encouraged to:

1.  Assume the leadership in establishing a climate of acceptance of the student teacher by faculty members and other school staff members.

2.  Assist the student teacher in the development of appropriate professional relationships with faculty, staff, students, and the community.

3.  Share the responsibility of supervising the student teacher if requested to do so by the cooperating teacher and/or university coordinator or supervisor by observing student's lessons and conduct a follow-up conference.

4.  Share with student teacher at the district's mentoring procedures if appropriate.

5.  Conduct a mock interview if requested.

# Observation and Evaluation of Student Teachers

*"In other words, if a teacher only teaches in one way, then they conclude that the kids who can't learn well that way or don't have the ability, when in fact, it may be that the way the teacher's teaching is not a particularly good method for the way the kids learn."*
—Robert Sternberg

# A. Evaluation, an Ongoing Process

The University of Northern Iowa's student teaching program is built around the concept of continuous evaluation. The cooperating teacher and the university coordinator or supervisor share in the continuous evaluation of the student teacher. Gathering and using information that will be helpful to the student teacher requires diligent professional attention. This evaluation begins with formal and informal observations of the student teacher in action. Through the use of a variety of data-collection tools, the university coordinator/supervisor and the cooperating teacher can collect objective information that can help the student teacher grow. Often, at the end of the observation, a formal or informal conference is held to discuss what has been observed with the student teacher.

## Conferencing

Systematically observing, analyzing, and reflecting on collected data and providing feedback to the student teacher are the most important responsibilities a cooperating teacher has during a student teaching experience. By meeting observation and conference responsibilities, the cooperating teacher helps the student teacher reflect on teaching effectiveness and the development of self-evaluation skills. The cooperating teacher should hold weekly conferences in addition to daily informal conversations. The university coordinator or supervisor should hold similar conferences before and after a formal observation. Information sharing between the cooperating teacher and the university coordinator or supervisor regarding the student teacher's progress is critical. Such communication can occur during three-way conferences, two-way conferences, or via telephone conversations.

The following tips will help ensure effective conferences.

1.  Observation notes, which can be used to stimulate recall of the student teacher's performance, are very beneficial.

2.  Each person approaches the conference open-mindedly, ready to share and listen to various viewpoints.

3.  Mutual trust and respect are maintained between those involved.

4.  Purposes for the conference are clearly identified.

5.  Progress from conference to conference is examined and discussed.

6.  Conferences are private and held away from the presence of pupils or other faculty. Confidentiality is professional and necessary for establishing the mutual trust and respect mentioned above.

7.  All conferences end on a positive note and, if necessary, with a plan of action the student teacher helped to develop.

# Feedback

Feedback is a critical way of helping another person change behaviors and improve skills. It is communication that gives the person information about how she/he affects others.

The following guidelines for effective feedback were adapted from Porter (1982).

1. Effective feedback describes a situation or a behavior. Statements that evaluate or judge performance tend to make the student teacher more defensive.

2. Feedback is most useful if provided soon after an observation has been made. Generally, feedback should be supplied immediately after a lesson or at the end of the day. In some instances the student teacher may need time to collect herself/himself after an upsetting experience. The observer will need to assess when the student teacher is ready to receive the feedback.

3. Feedback should be as specific and objective as possible. Script notes, audio and/or videotapes are excellent tools for providing feedback, which is objective and specific.

4. Feedback is a two-way interaction, and the needs of both parties must be considered. In providing feedback, the sender must keep in mind the needs of the receiver. Feedback that satisfies only the sender's needs can be both frustrating and destructive to the receiver.

5. Feedback is most useful when it is directed at behavior, which the receiver can influence or change. Frustration and resentment may occur when the student teacher is informed of shortcomings, which cannot be controlled.

6. The sender should check to be sure that the student teacher has understood the feedback. When feedback lacks clarity, misunderstandings may produce unintended results, which are counter-productive.

7. Asking honest questions, which are open-minded and encourage the student teacher to analyze feelings, beliefs and behaviors, may provide feedback. "Trick" questions or questions to which the observer already has an answer may undermine the trusting and supportive relationship needed for effective analysis of classroom events.

8. Feedback needs to reaffirm the student teacher's worth, competence, and ability to achieve success. Feedback is a way of giving help and is a primary tool in helping the student teacher grow. Throughout the whole supervisory conference cycle, the student teacher should be apprised of his/her progress and performance both verbally and in writing. These practices should facilitate the final evaluation process.

9. Cooperating teachers are encouraged to pay particular attention to the information on the midterm and final evaluations. It is extremely helpful to the continuous evaluation process if the cooperating teacher is fully aware of and understands all the evaluation criteria.

## Using a Stenographer's Book

The use of a stenographer book has proved to be beneficial for both the student teacher and the cooperating teacher. Often, each will think of a question or a suggestion that applies to a situation, but because there is no immediate, appropriate time to ask or discuss the situation, the thought is simply retained in our mind. Normally, however, this thought or question becomes lost somewhere during the day.

A steno book is a perfect place to write your comments or questions, or simply a note. The student teacher uses one side of the page and the cooperating teacher uses the other. Then at a free moment, or at the end of the day, the steno book can be reviewed by both the student teacher and the cooperating teacher and the suitable discussion can take place.

## Google Documents

In a technology-rich environment, the use of Google Documents affords this shared environment between the student teacher, cooperating teacher and the university coordinator/supervisor. These documents enable the fluid give and take of conversations surrounding the educational environment. Whatever the mode of communication, it is essential for the student teacher to continually reflect, ask questions, and propose ideas to the cooperating teacher so that the cooperating teacher can respond.

### Reference Listed

Porter, L. 1982. *Giving and Receiving Feedback; It Will Never Be Easy, But It Can Be Better.* In L. Porters and B. Mohr (eds.), <u>NTL Reading Book for Human Relations Training (7th ed.)</u>. Arlington, Virginia: NTL Institute, pp. 42–45.

# B. Addressing Student Teacher Performance Problems

The cooperating teacher and the university coordinator or supervisor have the responsibility to let student teachers know where they stand regarding the level of competency that is necessary for successful completion of the student teaching experience.

If competencies necessary for successful teaching are inadequate, they must be clearly identified for the student teacher as early in the program as possible. It is recommended that the university coordinator/supervisor utilize the teacher education Notice of Concern to provide the student teacher with due process. A **Notice of Concern** should be viewed as an opportunity to improve (see below). If problems are identified early and the student teacher is aware of them and accepts them as problems, a successful plan may be devised that should lead to necessary growth. The cooperating teacher should:

1. Return to co-teaching and co-planning.

2. Insist upon detailed daily planning and thorough long-range planning so that review and revision are possible.

3. Share ideas for methodology and procedures.

4. Be sure the student teacher is ready for each new activity. Transfer responsibility slowly as readiness is demonstrated.

5. Demonstrate effective teaching strategies as needed via one of the Co-Teaching Models.

6. Provide ongoing support and positive feedback.

7. Identify factors that limit the student teacher's performance. Collaboratively develop strategies to overcome them.

The university coordinator/supervisor and the cooperating teacher must ensure there will be *"no surprises"* for the student teacher at the end (final evaluation).

In a small number of cases, it is possible that the normal term of student teaching will not be sufficient to warrant a recommendation for teaching licensure. Inadequacy is likely to be determined if weaknesses exist in various areas. A number of the following characteristics could lead to a possible determination of inadequacy:

1. Personal deficiency (extreme timidity; immaturity; mental health problems; excessive tardiness, excessive absences; failure to establish workable personal relationships with pupils, teachers, and auxiliary school personnel).

2. Lack of organizational skills (ineffective planning; failure to meet responsibilities; unable to establish effective routines).

3. Lack of interest in teaching.

4. Inability to communicate effectively.

5. Inability to manage a classroom independently (pupils cooperate only through intervention by the cooperating teacher; student teacher has to ask for continued help).

6. Inability to work effectively with people (cannot cooperate with a cooperating teacher, university coordinator or supervisor; cannot establish rapport with pupils).

7. Inability to evaluate self (refuses to evaluate self or evaluation is out of line with reality).

8. Inability to structure the environment in such a way that learning occurs (no apparent change of learning behavior on the part of the students; failure to provide the proper techniques for the specific learning tasks).

9. Has little or no concept of function of a school (has not considered philosophy of education; does not understand the social context of the school environment; does not see the relationship or importance of the various elements of the school program).

10. Does not seem to possess the essential skills of teaching (knowledge of subject matter; questioning; utilization of media; knowledge of use of common techniques of instruction; concept of method).

11. **If a cooperating teacher or building administrator requests a student teacher be removed from a placement at anytime during the placement, the student teacher will be removed immediately. The student teacher will receive a No Credit (NC) and will have to pay for an additional 8-week placement.** The failure and/or removal from **two** student teaching placements will result in the student being unable to receive teacher licensure recommendation from the University of Northern Iowa.

## C. Notice of Concern (NOC)

To assist with performance problems, the University of Northern Iowa has developed a *Notice of Concern* that should be used to document performance concerns and/or withdrawal.

1. A Notification of Concern form is created on the student's UNITED page.

2. The student receives an e-mail alert of an NOC affording him/her due process.

3. An indicator appears on the Student Progress screen to show that the problem exists and could keep the student from continuing with their student teaching.

4. The student must take the initiative to correct the problem.

5. When the problem has been corrected, the indicator is removed.

6. If the problem is not taken care of and it becomes an issue, the student teaching coordinator should involve the Coordinator of Student Teaching.

7. If the problem results in removal of the student teacher from the classroom the student will receive No Credit for this placement, and will need to reapply for permission to continue with a new placement. This application is addressed to the Coordinators of Elementary/Secondary Education. (See form *Letter for Reapplication for Student Teaching* in the Section *Frequency Asked Questions and Forms.*)

8. The Coordinators of Elementary/Secondary Education will seek the advice of the Coordinator of Student Teaching, the Student Teaching Coordinator and may solicit information from additional personnel to make decisions regarding the student teacher's ability to remain in the teaching program and will recommend action.

9. The general operating policy is to reassign a student teacher to an alternative student teaching center. Should the student teacher not demonstrate success in the second assignment, he/she will not be given an additional placement and will not be recommended to the state for teaching licensure.

10. On occasion, a student teacher is unable to show sufficient promise as a teacher. When this does happen, it is necessary that he/she be counseled out of the teaching profession. In such instances, it is the responsibility of the university coordinator, in conjunction with the Coordinator of Student Teaching, to carry out this action. The Coordinators of Elementary/Secondary Education will be notified. The university coordinator will work with the cooperating teacher(s), and building administrator(s) when such an action is warranted.

11. A student teacher who receives an "unsatisfactory" in one or more categories in the final evaluation of the first placement will have a notice of concern filed by the university supervisor. A student teacher who receives an "unsatisfactory" in one or more categories in the final evaluation of the second placement will not receive credit for that 2nd placement. The student teacher may be able to repeat the second placement in another setting to improve their level of performance.

12. In extenuating situations, every attempt will be made to assure the student has due process. However, any student teacher who endangers a student or presents an unsafe or unacceptable environment in the classroom may be removed without prior notice.

13. In the event a student voluntary withdraws from student teaching, a Notice of Concern with be written to document this withdrawal and will explain the procedures should the student want to re-apply to student teach at a future time.

## D. Withdrawal/Removal of a Student Teacher from a Student Teaching Placement

In the event that a student teacher is counseled out of student teaching, or if the student teacher's behavior is such that he/she must be dropped from student teaching, or a student teaching placement, the following procedure is used:

## Withdrawal

A student who withdraws voluntarily from student teaching prior to the drop date designated by the registers office will receive a "W" (withdrawn). Any withdrawal will be documented with a Notice of Concern to provide a record of the reason for the withdrawal (Refer to C. Notice of Concern). A student who withdraws past this "drop date" will receive a "NC" (no credit).

## Removal

The student teacher may be removed from the classroom if: 1) a cooperating teacher or building administrator requests this removal; 2) the student teaching coordinator determines the student displays a lack of progress based on the evaluation form; 3) the student teacher endangers a student or presents an unsafe or unacceptable environment in the classroom. For these removals the student teacher will receive a No Credit (NC) and will have to pay for an additional 8 week placement. (The failure and/or removal from **two** student teaching placements will result in the student being unable to receive teacher licensure recommendation from the University of Northern Iowa.)

Any student removed from student teaching will be provided an exit conference and given written reasons for the removal and suggestions for remediation. Information from the exit conference will be included in a Notice of Concern. The University of Northern Iowa provides due process for the student teacher through the NOC process. Students who wish to appeal any decision must follow the procedures identified by the teacher education program.

## Reapplication

The applicant for student teaching who previously received a "W" or a "NC" grade in a single student teaching placement must apply in writing to the Coordinators of Elementary Teacher Education and Secondary Teacher Education for an additional student teaching placement. (see Section FAQs and Forms) Approval by the Coordinators of Elementary and Secondary Teacher Education is required for an additional placement. The Coordinators of Teacher Education shall, if deemed advisable, conduct a "staffing" and/or a personal conference with the student prior to reaching a decision about the reapplication.

## Special Situation

In special cases, it may be advisable and proper for a student to withdraw with credit (pass). The student teaching coordinator should recommend the number of credit hours to be awarded and justify the recommendation. If this course of action is considered, it should be discussed with the Head of the Department of Teaching and the Coordinator for Student Teaching prior to discussion of the credit possibility with the student. If the student teacher has enough credit hours, he/she can graduate from the University of Northern Iowa with a non-teaching degree in education.

## Student Decision Not to Withdraw

The student who is advised by the coordinator, principal, or cooperating teacher to "withdraw" may decide to continue. If the student is permitted to continue, he/she must be informed that the final evaluation will be based on demonstrated performance and that a "no credit" grade might still be awarded.

# E. Two-Week Progress Report

Student Teacher: _____

**Directions to cooperating teachers**: Please complete, discuss, and sign this form. Have your student teacher send or bring it to his/her coordinator or supervisor at the end of the second week of the student teaching experience.

**The student teacher has had the following experiences in the past two weeks: (Check all that apply.)**

_____ 1.  Observed and discussed observations with the cooperating teacher.

_____ 2.  Learned names of pupils in his or her classroom.

_____ 3.  Has read and discussed school policies and classroom policies.

_____ 4.  Has taken responsibility for some parts of the classroom routines.

_____ 5.  Has aided pupils during supervised study time.

_____ 6.  Has co-planned/co-taught 1–2 lessons.

_____ 7.  Has done some independent teaching in either a small-group or large-group setting.

_____ 8.  Is acquainted with neighbor or department faculty, the administration, and staff.

**Directions to cooperating teachers**: **Circle** the word(s) that best reflect your student teacher's characteristics at this time.

**The student teacher's:**

1.  Enthusiasm is (acceptable    needs improvement.)
2.  Punctuality is (acceptable    needs improvement.)
3.  Academic preparation is (acceptable    needs improvement.)
4.  Knowledge of lesson plans is acceptable or needs improvement.
5.  Rapport and personal relations with pupils are (acceptable    needs improvement.)
6.  Poise in a large group is (acceptable    needs improvement.)
7.  Oral grammar and written communication is (acceptable    needs improvement.)
8.  Cooperation with you and pupils is (acceptable    needs improvement.)
9.  Overall commitment to this assignment is (acceptable    needs improvement.)
10. Knowledge of technology's application for student learning and professional decision making is (acceptable    needs improvement.)
11. Attire is (acceptable    needs improvement.)

**Comments:**

**Signatures** _____    _____
               (Cooperating Teacher)                        (Student Teacher)

# F. Midterm Evaluation Procedures for Student Teachers

(See Later Sections for Early Childhood Student Teacher Midterm Evaluations)

After the two-week assessment comes the midterm evaluation. The midterm evaluation is held at approximately the midpoint of the student teacher's assignment for the expressed purpose of reviewing the student teacher's progress to that point, and for re-examining the expectations, goals, and experiences for the remainder of the student teaching assignment. During this meeting the student teacher is encouraged to ask questions about aspects of the evaluation, which may be unclear, and to make note of suggestions for improvement. Student teachers are also encouraged to evaluate themselves and generate their own ideas for the refinement of their skills.

The purpose of evaluation in student teaching is to identify the strengths and limitations of the student teacher with an aim toward the continual professional growth of the student teacher. Obviously, ongoing communication is vital to the evaluation process, but we must ultimately put our thoughts onto a formal marking system and into a formal, supportive narrative. As you work with your student teacher, please assess them as they are, namely, student teachers. Look at their strengths and limitations, but keep in mind they are not seasoned, veteran teachers. Do not compare them to that person, but rather to a student who is at his/her capstone experience.

The cooperating teacher plays a very significant role in the midterm evaluation. The cooperating teacher is responsible for examples of the student teacher's success as well as specific examples of areas for improvement. In advance of the meeting, it is helpful for the cooperating teacher to arrange a quiet meeting place. Faculty lounges are not suitable sites due to the private nature of the meeting.

If aspects of the evaluation process are unclear, the cooperating teacher should schedule a meeting with the university coordinator and/or supervisor prior to the midterm evaluation. The university coordinator and/or supervisor should assist in interpreting the evaluation criteria and in judging what is perceived to be a reasonable expectation for the student teacher. Prior to the midterm evaluation, the university coordinator and/or supervisor may request to meet with the cooperating teacher to discuss the evaluation.

When completing the midterm evaluation, keep in mind that the midterm evaluation is generally a **conservative** estimate of the student teacher's progress. Evaluations, which are unrealistically high or low, do little to encourage or challenge the student teacher. Student teachers should complete a careful examination of the evaluation criteria provided on the following pages. *Note: Midterm evaluations are part of the formative assessment of the student teaching experience and are not a part of the permanent student teaching record. Midterm evaluation forms can also be attained at http://www.uni.edu/coe/departments/office-student-field-experiences/information-faculty/supervisors*

The ten-item evaluation checklist is completed and shared with the student teacher at the midterm evaluation. Students are evaluated on each of the ten items on a scale that ranges from Not Applicable (NA), Minimal Evidence (ME), Beginning (B), Emerging (E), Proficient (P), and Advanced (A). When seeking placement of these marks, the cooperating teacher may use one of the accompanying rubrics to assist with the endeavor. The purpose of the accompanying rubrics is to provide a reference for the meaning of each performance level of the scale (i.e., minimal evidence, beginning, emerging, proficient, and advanced), and to strive toward consistency in the interpretation of the scale as it relates to each of the competencies/characteristics or personal qualities on the evaluation form. These competencies/characteristics or personal qualities are believed to be essential to effective teaching. *(Note: The items describing each category are not listed in any type of rank order, nor are the categories listed to assume one is more important than another.)*

The accompanying rubrics were collaboratively designed and field-tested in 2012–2013 by the UNI/OSFE faculty and PreK-12 public school faculty. These are based on national (InTASC) and state (Iowa Bureau of Licensure) standards, and provide specific, observable competencies in a developmental framework to address all five performance levels in each of the 10 categories. The developmental nature of the rubric encourages formative as well as summative assessment.

UNIversity of Northern Iowa
College of Education
Office of Student Field Experiences
Cedar Falls, IA 50614

**MIDTERM EVALUATION**
**OF**
**STUDENT TEACHING**

Name: _____

| Last | First | Middle/Maiden |

| Student ID Number | | Major |

| Grade Level(s) | Building(s) | School District |

| City | State | Zip Code |

| University Coordinator | Clinical Supervisor | Cooperating Teacher |

Office _____ | | Building

Phone     Area | Beginning and Ending Dates | Phone     Area

Evaluation Scale:  NA..Not Applicable; ME..Minimal Evidence;  B..Beginning; E..Emerging; P..Proficient; A..Advanced

Check the Appropriate Circle

## COMPETENCIES/CHARACTERISTICS

## PERFORMANCE LEVELS

| | | NA | ME | B | E | P | A |
|---|---|---|---|---|---|---|---|
| 1. | **Learner Development** Understands how learners grow and develop, recognizing that patterns of learning and development vary individually within and across the cognitive, linguistic, social, emotional, and physical areas; designs and implements developmentally appropriate and challenging learning experiences. | O | O | O | O | O | O |
| 2. | **Learning Differences** Uses understanding of individual differences and diverse cultures and communities to ensure inclusive learning environments that enable each learner to meet high standards. | O | O | O | O | O | O |
| 3. | **Learning Environments** Works with others to create environments that support individual and collaborative learning; encourages positive social interaction, active engagement in learning, and self motivation. | O | O | O | O | O | O |
| 4. | **Content Knowledge** Understands the central concepts, tools of inquiry, and structures of the discipline(s) and creates learning experiences that make the discipline accessible and meaningful for learners to assure mastery of content. | O | O | O | O | O | O |
| 5. | **Application of Content** Understands how to connect concepts and use differing perspectives to engage learners in critical thinking, creativity, and collaborative problem solving related to authentic local and global issues. | O | O | O | O | O | O |
| 6. | **Assessment** Understands and uses multiple methods of assessment to engage learners in their own growth, to monitor learner progress, and to guide teacher's and learner's decision making. | O | O | O | O | O | O |
| 7. | **Planning for Instruction** Plans instruction that supports every student in meeting rigorous learning goals; draws upon knowledge of content areas, curriculum, cross-disciplinary skills, and pedagogy, and knowledge of learners and community context. | O | O | O | O | O | O |
| 8. | **Instructional Strategies** Understands and uses a variety of instructional strategies to encourage learners to develop deep understanding of content and their connections; builds skills to apply knowledge in meaningful ways. | O | O | O | O | O | O |
| 9. | **Professional Learning and Ethical Practice** Engages in ongoing professional learning; uses evidence to continually evaluate own practice; adapts practice to meet needs of each learner. | O | O | O | O | O | O |
| 10. | **Leadership and Collaboration** Seeks appropriate leadership roles and opportunities to take responsibility for student learning; collaborates with learners, families, colleagues, to ensure learner growth and advance the profession. | O | O | O | O | O | O |

# STUDENT TEACHING EVALUATION GUIDE EXPANDED RUBRICS

## Standard #1: Learner Development

The teacher candidate understands how learners grow and develop, recognizing that patterns of learning and development vary individually within and across the cognitive, linguistic, social, emotional, and physical areas, designing and implementing developmentally appropriate and challenging learning experiences.

### Advanced

The teacher candidate respects learners' differences and values/solicits/includes input from others in understanding and supporting each learner's development. The teacher candidate displays the ability to regularly assess individual and group performance to modify or create instruction to meet the learners' needs in each area of development (cognitive, linguistic, social, emotional, and physical). Instruction is developmentally appropriate, building on learner's strengths, taking the needs of all learners into account. The teacher candidate identifies learning readiness, and understands how development in one area may affect performance in others. Lesson plans and instruction consistently provide evidence that the teacher candidate understands the role of language and culture in learning and is able to modify instruction to make language comprehensible and instruction relevant, accessible, and challenging.

### Proficient

The teacher candidate values/solicits the input and contributions of families and other professionals to enhance each learner's development. The teacher candidate is able to assess individual and group performance for design or modification. Lessons are developmentally appropriate and take into account the strengths, interests, and needs of each learner. Lesson plans and instruction indicate that the teacher candidate has an idea of how learners construct knowledge, acquire skills, and develop thinking processes. Most lessons suggest that the teacher candidate understands the role of language and culture in learning.

### Emerging

The teacher candidate generally values the input and contributions of families and other professionals for the development of learner's growth, but may not solicit this input. The teacher candidate is able to assess individual and/ or group performance for design or modification for most lessons, although the modifications may be global in nature, addressing class needs instead of the needs of the individual learners. The lessons are generally developmentally appropriate but may not account for the strengths, interests, and needs of all learners. The candidate understands that learners are at different levels of skills, abilities, and knowledge and works to adjust some lessons to meet those needs and abilities. Lessons suggest that the teacher candidate is attempting to include language and culture in learning.

### Beginning

The teacher candidate takes into consideration some of the feedback from colleagues or families and understands that modifications are needed. The teacher candidate respects learners' differences. The teacher candidate is beginning to understand how learners construct knowledge, acquire skills, and develop disciplined thinking processes. Although the teacher candidate is aware that language and culture influence learning, the teacher candidate is just beginning to incorporate this into some lessons.

### Minimal Evidence

The teacher candidate seldom seeks input or feedback from colleagues or families on learner development.. The teacher candidate designs lessons with preconceived outcomes, with little or no regard to student strengths, interests, or thinking processes. The teacher candidate may consider language and culture's influence on learning, but the follow through of this knowledge to lessons is weak.

# Standard #2: Learner Differences

The teacher candidate utilizes an understanding of individual differences, with rich diverse cultural and community backgrounds to ensure inclusive learning environments that enable each learner to meet high standards.

## Advanced

The teacher candidate believes all learners can achieve at high levels and persists in helping each learner reach his/her full potential. The teacher candidate designs, adapts, and delivers instruction to address each learner's diverse learning strengths and needs and creates opportunities for learners to demonstrate their understanding in different ways. The candidate understands and identifies differences among learners with exceptional needs: including English Language Learners, students with disabilities, and gifted students. The teacher candidate is able to access resources and support to advance all learner's growth.

## Proficient

The teacher candidate respects learners as individuals with differing personal and family backgrounds and various skills, abilities, perspectives, talents, and interests. The teacher candidate understands that learners bring assets for learning based on a variety of factors: including ability, talent, language, culture, and community values. The teacher candidate considers these elements when planning instruction, incorporating multiple perspectives into his/her lessons and makes them accessible for all language learners.

## Emerging

The teacher candidate respects learners and their full potential. The teacher candidate considers diverse learning styles and allows some learners to progress independently. The teacher candidate understands the importance of planning with multiple perspectives and is working on developing these skills.

## Beginning

The teacher candidate respects learners and acknowledges diverse learning strengths and needs when planning instruction, but lacks clear defined lessons to address these learner differences. Although some learners are allowed to progress independently, most are held to group activities and assignments. The teacher candidate may occasionally incorporate information about diverse cultures into lessons.

## Minimal Evidence

Although the teacher candidate demonstrates a respect for learners in general, there is little consideration of learners' diverse cultures or communities in the planning of the lessons. At the same time there is little to no consideration for the diverse strength and needs of the learner when the teacher candidate plans the lesson.

# Standard #3: Learning Environments

The teacher candidate works with others to create environments that support individual and collaborative learning, and that encourage positive social interaction, active learner engagement, and self-motivation.

## Advanced

The teacher candidate independently collaborates with learners, families, and colleagues to design lessons to engage learners in collaborative and self-directed learning. The teacher candidate and learners develop shared values and demonstrate respect for differing learner perspectives. New and unique activities are introduced to increase student engagement in the content and with other learners. Collaboration promotes interaction among learners and fosters peer relationships. Learning experiences are designed to build learner self-direction and to engage learners through interactive technologies to enhance a global perspective. Because the teacher candidate has created a learning environment where students are engaged and excited about learning, classroom management meets the needs of the students, is varied, and thoughtful.

## Proficient

The teacher candidate confidently collaborates with learners, families, and colleagues to provide a safe and positive learning climate that engages learners in collaborative learning. The teacher candidate utilizes a variety of methods to engage learners and communicates in a way that demonstrates respect for differing cultures and backgrounds. The classroom is designed to encourage collaborative peer relationships and cooperative learning environments. It is because of this student engagement that classroom management is active and positive. As much as possible, the teacher candidate uses interactive technologies to enhance and expand students' perspectives beyond the classroom.

## Emerging

The teacher candidate maintains a safe and positive learning climate for all learners. The teacher candidate utilizes a variety of methods that includes most learners and incorporates respect for individual differences in activities. The teacher candidate utilizes a variety of strategies for classroom management and is able to adjust to changing environments. The teacher candidate attempts to utilize technology and collaborative groupings occasionally, but this effort is not the norm.

## Beginning

The teacher candidate understands the importance of collaborative learning, but the efforts to engage learners in lessons utilizing this learning are few. The teacher candidate is successful when plans are made with help from the cooperating teacher to develop activities that increase engagement and recognizes the individual learner's perspective. Classroom management is formulaic and therefore is partially effective. Technology might be used for a lesson for research or production only.

## Minimal Evidence

The teacher candidate provides lessons that engage learners in large group response or individual work with little or no group collaboration. The instructional methods used show little variety. Classroom management is weak. Minimal use of interactive technology is demonstrated.

# Standard #4: Content Knowledge

The teacher candidate understands the central concepts, tools of inquiry, and structures of the discipline(s) he or she teaches and creates learning experiences that make these aspects of the discipline accessible and meaningful for learners to assure mastery of the content.

## Advanced

The teacher candidate consistently uses multiple representations to engage learners in a variety of experiences accommodating different learning styles to advance learner development. The teacher candidate realizes that content knowledge is complex, culturally situated, and ever evolving. The teacher candidate appreciates multiple perspectives within the discipline and facilitates learners' perspectives. The teacher candidate facilitates discussions that reflect on prior knowledge and link it to new information. The teacher candidate is able to recognize learner misconceptions, and is able to redirect and ensure accessibility and relevance for all learners through clear, accurate and substantive use of academic language. Instruction is created using best practices with the rich inclusion of culturally relevant content that provide perspectives in a global society.

## Proficient

The teacher candidate explains content using multiple representations to engage learners in experiences in order to understand diverse perspectives. The teacher candidate is current in content knowledge and appreciates multiple perspectives. The teacher candidate expects learners to reflect on prior knowledge and make links to new information. The teacher candidate is able to recognize learner misconceptions and is able to redirect and ensure accessibility and relevance for all learners through accurate use of academic language. Instruction includes culturally relevant content.

## Emerging

Teacher candidate uses more than one method of representation to engage learners in lessons. The teacher candidate is committed to advance each learner's mastery of disciplinary content and skills. Although lessons are linked to previous knowledge, these links are described by the teacher candidate but not always made by the learners. Proper academic language is used to encourage academic inquiry and analysis. The teacher candidate works to include culturally relevant content.

## Beginning

The teacher candidate attempts more than one method of representation to engage learners in lessons involving some inquiry or analysis of ideas. Even though the teacher candidate is generally current on content ideas and understandings he/she is only moderately successful at utilizing academic language. The teacher candidate understands the need to include culturally relevant content but struggles with its implementation.

## Minimal Evidence

The teacher candidate uses a single or outdated method of representation of content, and as a result, engages learners in lessons that are designed to deliver predestined content regardless of previous learning. Few if any links to previous knowledge of learners are provided by the teacher candidate. The teacher candidate struggles with content knowledge, which prevents the inclusion of culturally relevant content.

# Standard #5: Application of Content

The teacher candidate understands how to connect concepts and use different strategies to engage learners in critical thinking, creativity, and collaborative problem solving related to authentic local and global issues.

## Advanced

The teacher candidate incorporates creativity in designing lessons and requires learners to use creativity in collaborative problem solving amongst peers. Lessons include authentic issues that are relevant to learners while incorporating an effective level of scaffolding and modeling. Problem solving incorporates previously learned concepts and connects with new concepts to seek new and creative solutions to authentic situations. The teacher candidate is adept at utilizing technology to enhance learning in the content areas.

## Proficient

The teacher candidate provides learners with opportunities to think creatively and work collaboratively in problem solving during instructional activities. Lessons include authentic issues that are relevant to learners while incorporating an adequate level of scaffolding and modeling. The teacher candidate demonstrates questioning skills that help learners connect new content to prior learning and experiences. The teacher candidate understands and uses technology to learning in the content areas.

## Emerging

The teacher candidate asks learners to think creatively to solve problems with some time provided for collaborative work. Although some assignments include authentic local or global issues that depend on previous learning, links to this prior knowledge are partial. The teacher candidate's knowledge about the use to technology to advance content understanding is adequate, but lacks follow through to foster learning in the classroom.

## Beginning

The teaching candidate provides learners structured problem-solving strategies that result in a predetermined outcome. Issues are contrived or viewed from limited perspectives and generally do not connect with learners' prior learning or experiences. Questioning skills seldom go beyond recall or basic knowledge. The teacher candidate demonstrates limited knowledge of technology and/or its application to foster learning.

## Minimal Evidence

The teacher candidate provides limited opportunities for collaborative work, problem solving, or creativity. Concepts are provided as separate units of instruction lacking connections between content and prior learning experiences. Only one perspective is offered in planned lessons. The teacher candidate has weak knowledge of the use of technology in the classroom to foster learning.

# Standard #6: Assessment

The teacher candidate understands and uses multiple methods of formal and informal assessments to engage learners in their own growth, to monitor learner progress, and to guide the teacher's and learner's decision making.

## Advanced

The teacher candidate is able to create and implement multiple forms of both formative and summative assessments. The teacher candidate aligns the assessment methods with the learning objectives and uses the data from the assessments to help learners make decisions and become more responsible for their own learning. The teacher candidate makes sound decisions regarding future curricular materials and instruction based on assessment data. The teacher candidate is able to make meaningful accommodations in assessments and testing conditions to meet the needs of every learner.

## Proficient

The teacher candidate is able to create and implement both formative and summative assessments and is able to use the information to determine the appropriate steps to providing feedback and delivering instruction to learners. The teacher candidate involves learners in the decision-making process. The teacher candidate aligns assessment methods with the learning objectives and uses sensible approaches to make accommodations in the assessments and testing conditions to meet the needs of every learner.

## Emerging

The teacher candidate is able to use formative or summative assessments. Although the teacher candidate recognizes the importance of the data for deciding future course of action for learner, most assessment is used to monitor student performance. Assessment data is seldom shared with the learners to help them become engaged in their own growth. The teacher candidate only partially aligns assessment methods with the learning objectives. The teacher candidate assessment accommodations for different learners are simplistic.

## Beginning

The teacher candidate understands the importance of assessment and is starting to use formative as well as summative assessments for more than grading purposes. The teacher candidate's monitoring of learner progress utilizes mostly predesigned summative assessments. There is minimal accommodation on assessments for learner differences.

## Minimal Evidence

The teacher candidate uses commercially prepared assessments as a summative evaluation and moves on to the next unit of instruction with minimal feedback to learners. Assessment data is used for grading purposes only. The teacher candidate has not used assessments in a meaningful way, nor made any accommodations for learner differences.

# Standard #7: Planning for Instruction

The teacher candidate plans instruction to support every student in meeting rigorous learning goals by drawing upon knowledge of content areas, curriculum, cross-disciplinary skills, and pedagogy, as well as knowledge of learners and the community context.

## Advanced

The teacher candidate consistently demonstrates the ability to differentiate instruction based on the needs of the individual learners, and the contextual factors of the learning environment. Learning goals are tightly aligned with the curriculum and allow for rigorous expectations for all learners, including higher order thinking skills. Instruction is aligned to the skill level of each learner. The teacher candidate demonstrates in-depth content knowledge, the willingness to expand his/her repertoire of instructional strategies, and the ability to recognize and plans for cross-disciplinary opportunities.

## Proficient

The teacher candidate demonstrates the ability to differentiate instruction and content based on the needs of individual students. Learning goals are adequately aligned with the curriculum. Instruction is appropriate for the skill level of all learners. The teacher candidate demonstrates content knowledge; and the ability to use effective, appropriate instructional strategies and the ability to recognize cross-disciplinary opportunities.

## Emerging

The teacher candidate is attempting to differentiate instruction and/or differentiate content based on the needs of all learners. Some learning goals may be properly aligned with the curriculum. Athough there is limited use of instructional strategies, most instructional practices are directed towards the majority skill level of learners. The teacher candidate demonstrates sufficient content knowledge.

## Beginning

The teacher candidate provides sketchy differentiation for learners in content or instruction. Learning goals are minimally aligned with curriculum. The teacher candidate has routine content knowledge, and instruction is at the correct skill level for learners.

## Minimal Evidence

The teacher candidate provides little or no differentiation for learners. Many of the learning goals are missing or do not align with curriculum. The teacher candidate's content knowledge is inadequate, and instruction is unrelated to the skill level for learners.

# Standard #8: Instructional Strategies

The teacher candidate understands and uses a variety of instructional strategies to encourage learners to develop deep understanding of content areas and their connections, and to build skills to apply knowledge in meaningful ways.

## Advanced

The teacher candidate values, understands and applies a variety of instructional strategies while making well-defined differentiation for all learners. The teacher candidate engages learners in critical thinking activities. The teacher candidate is intentional about designing opportunities for learners to demonstrate their understanding through engagement in meaningful tasks.

## Proficient

The teacher candidate recognizes and applies a variety of instructional strategies while making appropriate differentiation for most learners. The teacher candidate provides adequate opportunities for learners to engage in critical thinking in content areas and works to make tasks meaningful.

## Emerging

The teacher candidate recognizes a variety of instructional strategies but utilizes only a few in instruction. Most of the instructional strategies are designed to help the class apply knowledge and demonstrate understanding through tasks, some of which are meaningful.

## Beginning

Although the teacher candidate recognizes several teaching strategies, he/she only applies the few that are comfortable to the teacher candidate. Some of these strategies help some of the learners understand the content area or to apply the knowledge.

## Minimal Evidence

The teacher candidate has weak understanding of a variety of instructional strategies and uses limited strategies to deliver content. These limited strategies are only partially effective in helping learners understand the content.

# Standard #9: Professional Learning and Ethical Practice

The teacher candidate engages in ongoing professional learning and uses evidence to continually evaluate his/her practice, particularly the effects of his/her choices and actions on others (learners, families, other professionals, and the community) and the uses of these practices to meet the needs of each learner.

## Advanced

The teacher candidate participates as a member of a professional learning community (school faculty) aimed at pulling together best practices for classroom instruction and methodology to improve student learning through the implementation of these practices into the classroom. This professional engagement is demonstrated through attendance at school professional development activities (e.g., workshops, seminars, webinars, or guest speakers) as well as other sources. Information garnered through professional learning opportunities is appropriately implemented into classroom instruction, methodology, or professional relationships as available. The teacher candidate demonstrates strong commitment to the profession through contributions to professional development.

## Proficient

The teacher candidate understands the importance of continued professional growth and seeks opportunities to further that knowledge of content, methodology, and school related topics. This professional engagement is demonstrated through attendance at school professional development activities (e.g., workshops, seminars, webinars, or guest speakers) as well as networking with other teachers to expand his/her practice. Through this involvement, the student teacher is able to make connections between professional development opportunities and the classroom. The teacher candidate understands and demonstrates the expectations of the profession.

## Emerging

The teacher candidate attends building provided professional development opportunities and engages in conversations pertaining to potential connections to classroom instruction. The teacher candidate is aware of the need to adapt practices and has begun to make the adaptations for special needs students. The teacher candidate positively demonstrates professionalism.

## Beginning

The teacher candidate attends building required professional development activities only. Little or no effort is demonstrated to make any connection with the implementation to classroom instruction.

## Minimal Evidence

The teacher candidate misses or avoids new personal learning opportunities. The teacher candidate is unaware of the needs and does not make adaptations to impact student achievement. The teacher candidate demonstrates unprofessional behavior, such as poor attendance, tardiness, inappropriate attire, unprofessional demeanor or interactions with students, parents, and/or education professionals.

# Standard #10: Leadership and Collaboration

The teacher candidate seeks appropriate leadership roles and opportunities to take responsibilities for student learning, to collaborate with learners, families, colleagues, other school professionals, and community members to ensure learner growth, and to advance the profession.

## Advanced

The teacher candidate takes an active role on the instructional team, giving and receiving feedback on practice, examining learner work, analyzing data from multiple sources, and sharing responsibility for decision making and accountability for each student's learning. Working with school colleagues, the teacher candidate builds ongoing connections with community resources to enhance student learning and well being for both face-to-face and virtual contexts. The teacher candidate appropriately models effective practice for colleagues, engages in professional learning activities, and serves in leadership roles. The candidate advocates for the needs of learners, to strengthen the learning environment, and understand system change. The teacher candidate takes responsibility for advancing the profession. The teacher candidate embraces the challenge of continuous improvement while taking responsibility for contributing to and advancing the profession.

## Proficient

The teacher candidate understands schools as organizations with a school culture and knows how to work with others across the system to support learners and the shared vision of the school. The teacher candidate knows how to work with other adults and has developed skills in collaborative interaction appropriate for both face-to-face and virtual contexts. The teacher candidate knows how to contribute to a common culture that supports high expectations for student learning. The teacher candidate works with other colleagues to plan and jointly facilitate learning on how to meet diverse needs of learners. The teacher candidate embraces the challenge of continuous improvement.

## Emerging

The teacher candidate is aware of the shared vision of the school. The teacher candidate understands that the alignment of family, school, and community enhances student learning, but may not be able to make active contributions to use this knowledge. Although the teacher candidate understands the importance of shared responsibility, the teacher candidate is only beginning to develop skills in collaborative interaction appropriate for both face-to-face and virtual contexts.

## Beginning

The teacher candidate has limited awareness of the shared vision of the school. The teacher candidate is beginning to understand that the alignment of family, school, and community enhances student learning. The teacher candidate collaborates with colleagues when asked and is making some progress towards developing skills in collaborative interaction appropriate for both face-to-face and virtual contexts.

## Minimal Evidence

The teacher candidate has no awareness of the shared vision of the school. The teacher candidate demonstrates only a vague understanding that the alignment of family, school, and community enhances student learning. The teacher candidate avoids collaboration with colleagues and makes little progress towards developing collaborative skills.

# G. Final Evaluation Procedures for Student Teachers

(See H & I Sections for Early Childhood Student Teachers)

The preparation of the final evaluation is an important responsibility. Time and careful thought should be given to this document. The final evaluation may become a part of the official credentials for prospective teachers. The university coordinator of student teaching and/or supervisor will provide instruction on how the final evaluation form is to be completed. There will be a final conference for the purpose of discussing the evaluation with the student teacher. The university coordinator, via the UNITED System, will assume final responsibility for submission of the student teaching evaluation to the student teacher's university record.

In evaluating a student teacher, the cooperating teachers are asked to indicate on the ten item scale that ranges from Not Applicable (NA), Minimal Evidence (ME), Beginning (B), Emerging (E), Proficient (P), and Advanced (A). When seeking placement of these marks, the cooperating teacher may use one of the accompanying rubrics to assist with the endeavor. The purpose of the accompanying rubrics is to provide a reference for the meaning of each performance level of the scale (i.e., minimal evidence, beginning, emerging, proficient, and advanced), and to strive toward consistency in the interpretation of the scale as it relates to each of the competencies/characteristics or personal qualities on the evaluation form. These competencies/characteristics or personal qualities are believed to be essential to effective teaching. Note: When evaluating, the cooperating teacher should think of their student teacher in terms of other teacher candidates at the completion of their student teaching experience. It is necessary to avoid comparing the student teacher to experienced teachers. While some are capable of teaching at a demonstrated level of master teacher, most will lack that level of experience.

## Writing the Narrative Section

The following guidelines are to assist you in preparing a narrative description of the student teacher's experience. As the narrative is written, consider the following ideas:

1. The performance rankings should be consistent with and supported by the written narrative.

2. The narrative should contain objective statements that are supported by specific descriptions. For example:

   *"Ms. Andrews effectively guided the pupils' learning of important concepts in content material. She carefully identified and taught the necessary vocabulary and prepared study guides which were used to stimulate discussion."*

3. Narrative statements are precise, descriptive, and should never be open to misinterpretation. The majority of the narrative should be written in *past tense* since the final evaluation comes at the end of the student teaching experience. *Future tense* should be used when making predictions of the student teacher's future potential as a classroom teacher.

The written evaluation should address the following areas but doesn't necessarily need to be in the suggested six-paragraph format. It is common to find written evaluations covering the same information in four or five paragraphs.

**Paragraph one—classroom setting**. This paragraph describes the environment. Information about the community and the school, the range of student abilities, the socio-economic background of the pupils, the setting in which the student teacher worked including the number of pupils, classes or subject matter, a description of the teaching responsibilities and extra duties may be included in this paragraph.

**Paragraph two—special skills and competencies**. Describe special skills that the student teacher possessed and demonstrated. For example: lesson planning, evaluating students' work, co-teaching and co-planning and carrying out worthwhile activities, incorporating a variety of learning styles into lessons, constructing bulletin boards and/or learning centers, etc. Anything that was done especially well should be emphasized.

**Paragraph three—classroom management**. Describe the student teacher's ability to establish rapport with pupils and how effective were her/his classroom management skills.

**Paragraph four—areas needing improvement**. *(Optional)* Describe any weaknesses that the student teacher possesses. Also reflect on the student teacher's ability to correct said weak areas and offer a prediction of the success of the student teacher in achieving correction of the same.

**Paragraph five—character and personality**. Describe any professional characteristic(s) that might make this student a good beginning teacher (reflective, personable, dedicated, responsible, hard working, conscientious, energetic, intelligent, open to constructive feedback, ebullient, maintains a professional appearance, etc.). Discuss how the student teacher related to you, the cooperating teacher; administration; staff and parents.

**Paragraph six—prediction for success**. Give a professional opinion as to the probable success of this student teacher based on personal growth and professional development shown throughout the student teaching experience.

The length of the final narrative should be approximately 400–500 words. However, if more is necessary to reflect the student teacher's performance, then more narrative should be written. *(Note: Final evaluation forms can also be attained at <u>http://www.uni.edu/coe/departments/office-student-field-experiences/ information-faculty/supervisors</u>*

UNIversity of Northern Iowa
College of Education
Office of Student Field Experiences
Cedar Falls, IA 50614

**FINAL EVALUATION
OF
STUDENT TEACHING**

Name: _____

| Last | First | Middle/Maiden |

Student ID Number                                    Major

Grade Level(s)                    Building(s)                    School District

City                              State                          Zip Code

University Coordinator            Clinical Supervisor            Cooperating Teacher

Office _____                                   Building _____

Phone    Area              Beginning and Ending Dates            Phone    Area

---

Evaluation Scale:  NA..Not Applicable; ME..Minimal Evidence;  B..Beginning; E..Emerging; P..Proficient; A..Advanced        Check the Appropriate Circle

| COMPETENCIES/CHARACTERISTICS | PERFORMANCE LEVELS | | | | | |
|---|---|---|---|---|---|---|
| | NA | ME | B | E | P | A |
| **1. Learner Development** Understands how learners grow and develop, recognizing that patterns of learning and development vary individually within and across the cognitive, linguistic, social, emotional, and physical areas; designs and implements developmentally appropriate and challenging learning experiences. | O | O | O | O | O | O |
| **2. Learning Differences** Uses understanding of individual differences and diverse cultures and communities to ensure inclusive learning environments that enable each learner to meet high standards. | O | O | O | O | O | O |
| **3. Learning Environments** Works with others to create environments that support individual and collaborative learning; encourages positive social interaction, active engagement in learning, and self motivation. | O | O | O | O | O | O |
| **4. Content Knowledge** Understands the central concepts, tools of inquiry, and structures of the discipline(s) and creates learning experiences that make the discipline accessible and meaningful for learners to assure mastery of content. | O | O | O | O | O | O |
| **5. Application of Content** Understands how to connect concepts and use differing perspectives to engage learners in critical thinking, creativity, and collaborative problem solving related to authentic local and global issues. | O | O | O | O | O | O |
| **6. Assessment** Understands and uses multiple methods of assessment to engage learners in their own growth, to monitor learner progress, and to guide teacher's and learner's decision making. | O | O | O | O | O | O |
| **7. Planning for Instruction** Plans instruction that supports every student in meeting rigorous learning goals; draws upon knowledge of content areas, curriculum, cross-disciplinary skills, and pedagogy, and knowledge of learners and community context. | O | O | O | O | O | O |
| **8. Instructional Strategies** Understands and uses a variety of instructional strategies to encourage learners to develop deep understanding of content and their connections; builds skills to apply knowledge in meaningful ways. | O | O | O | O | O | O |
| **9. Professional Learning and Ethical Practice** Engages in ongoing professional learning; uses evidence to continually evaluate own practice; adapts practice to meet needs of each learner. | O | O | O | O | O | O |
| **10. Leadership and Collaboration** Seeks appropriate leadership roles and opportunities to take responsibility for student learning; collaborates with learners, families, colleagues, to ensure learner growth and advance the profession. | O | O | O | O | O | O |

# Some Evaluative Qualities of Student Teachers

Use these suggested qualities as guides when writing your narrative portion of the student teacher final evaluation.

Organizational ability

Cooperation with professional staff

Ability to establish rapport with staff

Classroom management

Ability to write good lesson plans

Ability to relate content to students

Responses to suggestions

Utilization of media/technology

Creativity

Adaptability

Speech: speed, tone, volume, language usage

Understanding of students

Sense of humor

Questioning skills

Appearance

Enthusiasm

Ability to motivate students

Well rounded background

Ability to develop and use objectives

Recognizes individual differences

Pacing of class activity

Ability to anticipate problem areas

Ability to evaluate self

Strong professional ethics

Correct pronunciation of names

Respect for difference

Mediating conflict

Confidence

Tact

Empathy

Promptness

Initiative

Cultural awareness

Technological skills

Computer literacy

Conceptualization

Dependability

Motivated

Positive role model

Facilitates home/school relations

Awareness of service learning

Responsibility

Professional relations

# H. Midterm Evaluation Procedures for Early Childhood Student Teachers

After the two-week assessment, a midterm evaluation is conducted. The midterm evaluation is held at approximately the midpoint of the student teacher's assignment to review the student teacher's progress. This is done to re-examine the expectations, goals, and experiences for the remainder of the student teaching assignment. During this meeting, the student teacher is encouraged to ask questions about aspects of the evaluation that may be unclear and to make note of suggestions for improvement. Also, student teachers are also encouraged to evaluate themselves and to generate their own ideas for the refinement of their skills.

The purpose of evaluation in student teaching is to identify the strengths and limitations of the student teacher with an aim toward the continual professional growth of the student teacher. Obviously, ongoing communication is vital to the evaluation process, but we must ultimately put our thoughts onto a formal marking system and into a formal, supportive narrative. As you work with your student teacher, please assess them as they are, namely, student teachers. Look at their strengths and limitations, but keep in mind they are not seasoned, veteran teachers. Do not compare them to that person, but rather to a student who is at his/her capstone experience.

The cooperating teacher plays a very significant role in the midterm evaluation. The cooperating teacher is responsible for examples of the student teacher's success as well as specific examples of areas for improvement. In advance of the meeting, it is helpful for the cooperating teacher to arrange a quiet meeting place. Faculty lounges are not suitable sites due to the private nature of the meeting.

If aspects of the evaluation process are unclear, the cooperating teacher should schedule a meeting with the university coordinator and/or supervisor prior to the midterm evaluation. The university coordinator and/or supervisor should assist in interpreting the evaluation criteria and in judging what is perceived to be a reasonable expectation for the student teacher. Prior to the midterm evaluation, the university coordinator and/or supervisor may request to meet with the cooperating teacher to discuss the evaluation.

The fifteen (15)-item evaluation checklist is completed and shared with the student teacher at the midterm evaluation. Students are evaluated on each of the fifteen items on a scale. Scores (in order from least to most important) are unsatisfactory (U), low competent (LC), competent (CO), high competent (HC), or outstanding (O). When seeking placement of these marks, the cooperating teacher may use one of the accompanying rubrics to assist with the endeavor. The purpose of the accompanying rubrics is to provide a reference for the meaning of each performance level of the scale (i.e., unsatisfactory, low degree of competence, competent, high degree of competence, and outstanding), and to strive toward consistency in the interpretation of the scale as it relates to each of the competencies/characteristics or personal qualities on the evaluation form. These competencies/characteristics or personal qualities are believed to be essential to effective teaching. *(Note: The items describing each category are not listed in any type of rank order, nor are the categories listed to assume one is more important than another.)*

The accompanying rubrics are of two models. The first is a modified rubric where only the "outstanding," "competent," and "unsatisfactory" levels are described. The "high" and "low" levels of competency are somewhere in-between the bordering performance levels and should definitely be considered in the evaluation process. The second student teaching assessment rubric is modeled after the student teaching assessment rubric (STAR) which is based on national (INTASC) and state (Iowa Bureau of Licensure) standards, and provides specific, observable competencies in a developmental framework to address all five performance levels in each of the 15 categories. The developmental nature of the rubric encourages formative as well as summative usage.

When completing the midterm evaluation, keep in mind that the midterm evaluation is generally a conservative estimate of the student teacher's progress. Evaluations that are unrealistically high or low do little to encourage or challenge the student teacher. Student teachers should complete a careful examination of the evaluation criteria provided on the following pages. *Note: Midterm evaluations are part of the formative assessment of the student teaching experience and are not a part of the permanent student teaching record. Note: Midterm evaluation forms can also be attained at http://www.uni.edu/coe/ departments/office-student-field-experiences/information-faculty/supervisors.*

UNIversity of Northern Iowa
College of Education
Office of Student Field Experiences
Cedar Falls, IA 50614

**MIDTERM EVALUATION**
**OF**
**EARLY CHILDHOOD  STUDENT TEACHING**

Name: _____
Last                                          First                                          Middle/Maiden

_____
Student ID Number                                          Major

_____
Grade Level(s)                          Building(s)                          School District

_____
City                          State                          Zip Code

_____
University Coordinator          Clinical Supervisor          Cooperating Teacher

Office          _____          _____          Building
Phone          Area                          Beginning and Ending Dates          Phone          Area

Evaluation Scale:  U...Unsatisfactory;  CO...Competent;  HC...Highly Competent;  O...Outstanding          Check the Appropriate Circle

| COMPETENCIES/CHARACTERISTICS | PERFORMANCE LEVELS | | | | |
| --- | --- | --- | --- | --- | --- |
| | U | LC | CO | HC | O |
| 1. **Knowledge of Care-Giving and Skills Areas** Understands the central concepts of nurturing and care-giving; understands ages and stages of early childhood; plans and prepares nutritious foods when appropriate. | O | O | O | O | O |
| 2. **Knowledge of Learners and Learning Process** Understands how children learn and differ in their approaches to learning; provides learning opportunities and experiences that are meaningful and that support their development cognitively, socially, emotionally, physically and culturally; understands learners as a group and as individuals. | O | O | O | O | O |
| 3. **Instructional Planning** Plans instruction with children's health and safety as priority; understands, develops and implements curriculum based on knowledge of subject matter, students' interests, developmental levels, the community, state/district/accreditation standards, and curriculum goals. | O | O | O | O | O |
| 4. **Use of Instructional Strategies** Understands and uses a variety of instructional strategies; adapts teaching, curriculum, and care-giving styles to the diverse needs of students; understands and uses an appropriate balance between indirect and direct instruction; recognizes and capitalizes on teachable moments. | O | O | O | O | O |
| 5. **Learning Environment** Creates a safe and healthy learning environment that encourages positive social interaction, active engagement in learning and self-motivation; fosters independence through accessible materials and toys; demonstrates a positive, enthusiastic attitude toward learners and the task of teaching; able to recognize unsafe situations and act upon them in a timely fashion. | O | O | O | O | O |
| 6. **Classroom Management** Creates a fair, respectful, positive environment; sets clear expectations and reasonable consequences; uses both direct and indirect guidance techniques to encourage appropriate positive personal behavior choices; honors children's choices when appropriate; able to treat each child with dignity and as an individual. | O | O | O | O | O |
| 7. **Use of Communication Strategies** Uses knowledge of both oral, and non-verbal communication techniques to foster active inquiry, collaboration and supportive interactions that are developmentally appropriate. | O | O | O | O | O |
| 8. **Use of Assessing/Diagnosing/Evaluating Strategies** Understands and uses a variety of formal, informal, and authentic assessment strategies that align with instructional approaches; takes actions to determine what strengths and problems exist and responds appropriately to the assessment results; evaluates in an objective manner. | O | O | O | O | O |
| 9. **Use of Motivational Strategies** Uses multiple techniques, materials, and settings to kindle and sustain interest of learners; motivates by personal behavior; able to identify interest and non-interest behaviors and respects them. | O | O | O | O | O |
| 10. **Use of Problem-Solving/Decision Making Strategies** Reflects on teaching during and after lessons in order to recognize and solve problems and make decisions; examines situations from various perspectives and is appropriately decisive; able to seek out information from others and other sources to solve instructional or behavioral problems. | O | O | O | O | O |
| 11. **Home-School-Community Relations** Fosters relationships with colleagues, parents, and, as needed, agencies in the larger community. | O | O | O | O | O |
| 12. **Use of Technology** Integrates the computer and other high- and low-technology into preparation, classroom teaching activites, assessment and/or documentation. | O | O | O | O | O |
| 13. **Use of Multicultural Gender Fair (MCGF) Strategies** Demonstrates sensitivity to family, community diversity and cultural identity; infuses MCGF strategies into all professional interactions. | O | O | O | O | O |
| 14. **Human Relations Skills** Implements sound human relations and communication skills in order to foster productive, positive learning communities. | O | O | O | O | O |
| 15. **Professional Characteristics and Leadership** Exhibits high quality characteristics in professional and personal demeanor; professional behavior exemplifies role awareness and ethical conduct; takes initiative, recognizes and functions in the role of leader, or as an integral part of the staff, and takes on the appropriate role at the required time. | O | O | O | O | O |

# EARLY CHILDHOOD STUDENT TEACHING EVALUATION GUIDE: EXPANDED GUIDELINES

## Category 1: Knowledge of Care-Giving and Skills Areas

Understands the central concepts of nurturing and care-giving; understands ages and stages of early childhood; plans and prepares nutritious foods when appropriate.

## Outstanding

Anticipates physical, cognitive, affective, and linguistic needs and meets them with empathy and individuality. Demonstrates extensive content knowledge, seeks out additional information. Presents meaningful lessons based on human growth knowledge and continually reinforces them. Plans and implements high quality nutritious activities regularly into the curriculum and is conscientious about carrying out safe and hygienic procedures.

## High Degree of Competence

### Competent

Recognizes physical, cognitive, affective, and linguistic needs and attempts to meet the needs. Displays basic content knowledge; seeks out additional information. Uses human growth knowledge to develop an effective lesson. Prepares nutritious food using safe and hygienic procedures.

## Low Degree of Competence

### Unsatisfactory

Is unable to recognize the physical, cognitive, affective, and linguistic needs of the students. Demonstrates inaccurate or incomplete content knowledge, shows little or no effort to expand knowledge. Is unable to use human growth knowledge in the development of a lesson. Uses unsafe preparation, displays ignorance or disdain for nutritional needs of students.

|  | U | | CO | | O |
|---|---|---|---|---|---|
| MIDTERM EVALUATION......................... | | | | | |
| FINAL EVALUATION ............................... | | | | | |

# Category 2. Knowledge of Learners and Learning Process

Understands how children learn and differ in their approaches to learning; provides learning opportunities and experiences that are meaningful and that support their development cognitively, socially, emotionally, physically, and culturally; understands learners as a group and as individuals.

## Outstanding

Teaches lessons and activities with all students' needs and interests considered. Displays flexibility in planning and implementing complex and challenging experiences based on students' cognitive needs. Demonstrates consistent application of theories. Inspires pupils to think logically and reserve decisions until all evidence has been examined. Is consistently able to ascertain all pupils' needs.

## High Degree of Competence

### Competent

Develops and teaches lessons and activities with the group's needs considered. Plans challenging and complex lessons and activities that are developed for the group's cognitive needs and some individuals' cognitive needs. Demonstrates basic application of theories. Consistently alerts pupils to importance of logical thinking and decision making. Demonstrates basic ability to ascertain some of the pupils' needs.

## Low Degree of Competence

### Unsatisfactory

Develops and teaches lessons and activities that lack consideration of students' needs and interests. Develops lessons and activities that are taught without consideration of students' cognitive levels. Displays no application or inaccurate application of theories. Lacks demonstrated ability to lead pupils toward logical thinking or decision making. Demonstrates no interest, skills, or ability in ascertaining needs.

|  | U | CO | O |
|---|---|---|---|
| MIDTERM EVALUATION............................ | | | |
| FINAL EVALUATION ................................. | | | |

# Category 3.  Instructional Planning

Plans instruction with children's health and safety as priority; understands, develops, and implements curriculum based on knowledge of subject matter, students' interests, developmental levels, the community, state/district/accreditation standards, and curriculum goals.

## Outstanding

Is consistently diligent about planning for health and safety issues and anticipates and preempts unsafe situations. Demonstrates well-developed short- and long-range planning. Demonstrates clear purpose, organization, detail, flexibility, and alignment with standards: provides for individuality. Consistently exceeds planning and preparation deadlines. Consistently plans independently; shares drafted plans with C. T. for feedback. Consistently supplements prepared materials and organizes well. Solicits and takes students' interests and purposes into account when planning curriculum.

## High Degree of Competence

### Competent

Generally plans for health and safety issues. Demonstrates basic short- and long-range planning. Demonstrates clear purpose, organization, sufficient detail, and alignment with standards. Usually meets planning and preparation deadlines. Plans many lessons independently. Is able to acquire and organize prepared materials.

## Low Degree of Competence

### Unsatisfactory

Does not plan for health and safety factors; displays ignorance for health and safety issues. Demonstrates no short- or long-range planning. Demonstrates unclear purpose, organization, detail, and lack of alignment with standards. Does not meet planning or preparation deadlines. Totally relies on C. T. to plan. Has difficulty acquiring and organizing materials.

|  | U | CO | O |
|---|---|---|---|
| MIDTERM EVALUATION............................ | | | |
| FINAL EVALUATION ................................. | | | |

# Category 4. Use of Instructional Strategies

Understands and uses a variety of instructional strategies; adapts teaching, curriculum, and care-giving styles to the diverse needs of students; understands and uses an appropriate balance between indirect and direct instruction; recognizes and capitalizes on teachable moments.

## Outstanding

Displays well-developed teaching/care-giving style; consistently adjusts to student needs. Evaluates achievement based on course goals and objectives. Evidences use of fluent transition statements; makes transitions relevant to learning and to appear natural. Consistently paces instruction effectively. Delivers content in a manner that facilitates active learning. Constructs and manages an environment that provides for maximum student participation and response. Is always prompt and appropriate in responding to students: anticipates questions, discoveries, and needs.

## High Degree of Competence

### Competent

Sometimes adjusts teaching/care-giving style to students' needs. Makes good use of objectives in accompanying materials when setting goals. Understands and attempts to use transition statements that are relevant to learning and move the lesson fluently. Sometimes paces instruction effectively. Presents content clearly: attempts to make content relevant to students. Attempts to elicit maximum participation and response. Is sometimes prompt and always appropriate in responding to students.

## Low Degree of Competence

### Unsatisfactory

Rarely adapts teaching/care-giving style, or relies on only one teaching/care-giving style. Sets unclear or inappropriate goals and objectives. Uses transition statements that are inconsistent and ineffective. Demonstrates ineffective pacing. Is unable to present content in an effective manner. Does not plan for or effectively use pupil participation and response. Often ignores students or responds inappropriately.

|  | U |  | CO |  | O |  |
|---|---|---|---|---|---|---|
| MIDTERM EVALUATION............................ |  |  |  |  |  |  |
| FINAL EVALUATION.................................. |  |  |  |  |  |  |

# Category 5.  Learning Environment

Creates a safe and healthy learning environment that encourages positive social interaction, active engagement in learning and self-motivation; fosters independence through accessible materials and toys; demonstrates a positive, enthusiastic attitude toward learners and the task of teaching; able to recognize unsafe situations and act upon them in a timely fashion.

## Outstanding

Displays and implements sensitivity to the safe psychological needs and encourages perspective taking by the students. Facilitates students' desire to maintain a sound classroom climate. Makes a variety of materials and toys accessible for use and clean up by children; supplies toys and materials in anticipation of students' needs; encourages children to choose toys and materials and develops new materials for their use. Displays enthusiasm and positive attitude in all aspects of teaching even in stressful situations; facilitates students' desire to maintain a positive climate.

## High Degree of Competence

### Competent

Implements a psychologically safe, positive, and encouraging classroom. Maintains a positive classroom climate; experiences few instances of negativism. Makes an adequate number of materials and toys accessible for use and clean up by children. Displays pleasure in the children and teaching.

## Low Degree of Competence

### Unsatisfactory

Is unaware of psychologically safe strategies. Is not yet able to implement a sound classroom climate. Makes no effort to make materials and toys accessible. Displays a negative attitude about teaching and children.

|  | U | CO | O |
|---|---|---|---|
| MIDTERM EVALUATION | | | |
| FINAL EVALUATION | | | |

# Category 6. Classroom Management

Creates a fair, respectful, positive environment; sets clear expectations and reasonable consequences; uses both direct and indirect guidance techniques to encourage appropriate positive personal behavior choices; honors children's choices when appropriate; able to treat each child with dignity and as an individual.

## Outstanding

Effectively models fairness and equity and encourages students to exhibit fairness and equity in classroom. Is consistent and clear in establishing and monitoring expectations and student accountability. Consistently implements classroom management techniques to stimulate learning environment. Anticipates guidance problems; preventively implements effective, appropriate guidance techniques. Has learned to manage routine procedure; is able to adjust for non-routine needs. Anticipates and provides opportunities for student choice; honors the appropriate decisions and renegotiates the inappropriate ones.

## High Degree of Competence

### Competent

Takes an unbiased approach to classroom interactions. Sets standards and strives to consistently hold students accountable for their work and behavior. Is sometimes able to apply effective classroom management. Implements appropriate guidance techniques that produce desired results. Seeks help in planning some specific classroom procedures. Provides opportunities for students to choose desired behaviors and activities.

## Low Degree of Competence

### Unsatisfactory

Shows bias or uses statements that result in unfairness. Rarely establishes expectations or holds students accountable. Is unable to maintain adequate classroom management. Is unsuccessful in resolving guidance problems. Demonstrates little or no procedural management. Makes all decisions for students.

|  | U |  | CO |  | O |  |
|---|---|---|---|---|---|---|
| MIDTERM EVALUATION............................ | | | | | | |
| FINAL EVALUATION ................................. | | | | | | |

# Category 7. Use of Communication Strategies

Uses knowledge of both oral and non-verbal communication techniques to foster active inquiry, collaboration, and supportive interactions that support language development and are developmentally appropriate.

## Outstanding

Effectively varies vocal cues, rate, volume, and enunciation. Consistently demonstrates varied, advanced questioning techniques. Demonstrates mastery of standard English: is fluent, clear, expressive. Models depth and subtlety in interpersonal communication with students. Is organized; uses excellent spelling, grammar, mechanics, and overall style. Uses non-verbal communication; elicits natural, reciprocal communication. Consistently models and teaches appropriate usage of subject matter language.

## High Degree of Competence

### Competent

Uses a pleasant, well-modulated voice with adequate projection. Demonstrates varied, basic questioning techniques. Demonstrates basic competence in standard English. Usually communicates effectively with students. Is organized; proofs carefully to correct most spelling, grammar, and mechanics. Shows basic competence in non-verbal communication that supports verbal cues.

## Low Degree of Competence

### Unsatisfactory

Uses a weak, monotonous, or unexpressive voice. Does not demonstrate varied, basic questioning techniques. Makes frequent errors, grammatical mistakes, or uses inappropriate language for school setting. Lacks clarity in making explanations, fails to communicate effectively with students. Is disorganized or displays problems with spelling, grammar, or mechanics. Uses negative, conflicting, or distracting non-verbal communication or mannerisms.

|  | U | | CO | | O |
|---|---|---|---|---|---|
| MIDTERM EVALUATION | | | | | |
| FINAL EVALUATION | | | | | |

# Category 8. Use of Assessing/Diagnosing/Evaluating Strategies

Understands and uses a variety of formal, informal, and authentic assessment strategies that align with instructional approaches; takes actions to determine what strengths and problems exist and responds appropriately to the assessment results; evaluates in an objective manner.

## Outstanding

Develops varied authentic progress assessments that set the stage for re-teaching and individual remediation. Assesses understanding accurately; consistently responds to results by providing individual and group assistance and seeks out other resources. Is clear and consistent in communicating progress to parents in both formal and informal settings. Consistently maintains needed records; designs flexible systems as needed.

## High Degree of Competence

### Competent

Works to get beyond pre-existing formal assessments; uses assessments objectively. Provides adequate activities to assess formative understanding and monitors pupil progress; plans additional teaching based on assessment results. Is usually clear and consistent in communicating progress to parents in an informal setting. Usually maintains adequate records.

## Low Degree of Competence

### Unsatisfactory

Is unable to develop appropriate assessments or utilize pre-existing assessments effectively. Bases evaluation on traditional criteria with little or no understanding of the limitations of these procedures. Is often unclear, ineffective, or inconsistent in communicating progress to students and parents. Does not maintain adequate records.

|  | U | | CO | | O | |
|---|---|---|---|---|---|---|
| MIDTERM EVALUATION | | | | | | |
| FINAL EVALUATION | | | | | | |

# Category 9. Use of Motivational Strategies

Uses multiple techniques, materials, and settings to kindle and sustain interest of learners; motivates by personal behavior; able to identify interest and non-interest behaviors and respects them.

## Outstanding

Maintains pupil interest; experiences few discipline problems, even in challenging circumstances. Consistently establishes a stimulating environment, even in challenging circumstances. Consistently kindles students' interest by a variety of motivational strategies; uses challenging circumstances to enhance learning; participates in activities with genuine enthusiasm. Displays a proactive influence on motivation; recognizes and uses student motivations to plan before, during, and after lessons to better reach the students at their levels; uses the teachable moment effectively.

## High Degree of Competence

### Competent

Maintains pupil interest; experiences few discipline problems in routine circumstances. Often establishes a stimulating environment in typical circumstances. Integrates motivational activities and personal enthusiasm into standard curricular materials. Displays accurate recognition of student motivational levels; works to motivate students in activities.

## Low Degree of Competence

### Unsatisfactory

Shows inadequacy in maintaining pupil interest; struggles with discipline problems that result. Has difficulty establishing a stimulating environment. Uses unimaginative or inappropriate motivational activities; shows little or no enthusiasm for teaching or students. Underestimates importance of motivation and forces participation.

|  | U | CO | O |
|---|---|---|---|
| MIDTERM EVALUATION........................... | | | |
| FINAL EVALUATION................................. | | | |

# Category 10. Use of Problem-Solving/Decision-Making Strategies

Reflects on teaching during and after lessons in order to recognize and solve problems and make decisions; examines situations from various perspectives and is appropriately decisive; able to seek out information from others and other sources to solve instructional or behavioral problems.

## Outstanding

Consistently reflects accurately, sensitively, and thoroughly about his/her teaching. Displays advanced independent thinking and problem finding/solving skills; thoroughly examines needs and resources available and shares decisions/rationale with C. T. if necessary. Welcomes viewpoints of others, knows when to elicit them, and considers them before making final decisions. Easily fits materials and actions to situations, communicates decisions to others involved, and follows up independently. Consistently raises questions and actively researches alternatives to solve instructional problems or to find answers to educational questions.

## High Degree of Competence

### Competent

Is able to reflect on obvious issues or concerns regarding his/her teaching. Is developing independent thinking and problem finding/solving skills; makes decisions through discussion with C. T. Often considers viewpoints of others before making final decisions. Collects and organizes materials to support decisions. Raises questions about the merit of various solutions to problems and may attempt to research alternatives.

## Low Degree of Competence

### Unsatisfactory

Is unable to reflect during or after lessons. Demonstrates little independent thinking or strength of own opinion in problem finding/solving; relies on C. T. for decisions. Is reluctant to consider viewpoints of others before making final decisions. Is overly dependent; relies on others to follow up on decisions; is unwilling to follow up. Is reluctant to investigate or seek solutions to problems.

|  | U | CO | O |
|---|---|---|---|
| MIDTERM EVALUATION | | | |
| FINAL EVALUATION | | | |

# Category 11. Home-School-Community Relations

Fosters relationships with colleagues, parents, and, as needed, agencies in the larger community.

## Outstanding

Has become an integral part of the school staff by sharing information and responsibilities. Actively involves parents/guardians as part of child's total educational experience. Understands the value of accurate, continual communication with parents/guardians; able to lead a conference and demonstrates the ability to be tactfully honest. Takes initiative for contact and follow-up with community resources.

## High Degree of Competence

### Competent

Is able to work with colleagues on a routine basis. Regularly contacts parents/guardians on class or individual basis. Understands conferencing skills; supports the C. T. with information during conferences. Works with C. T. to involve community resources.

## Low Degree of Competence

### Unsatisfactory

Avoids working with colleagues. Fails to see value of contact or avoids family contact. Sees no value in communicating with parents/guardians; is unwilling to participate in conferences with C. T. Avoids contact with community resources.

|  | U | CO | O |
|---|---|---|---|
| MIDTERM EVALUATION.......................... | | | |
| FINAL EVALUATION................................ | | | |

# Category 12. Use of Technology

Integrates the computer and other high- and low-technology into preparation for teaching, classroom teaching activities, assessment, and/or documentation.

## Outstanding

Is proficient in location of software to meet individual, class, and teacher needs. Is proficient in locating high- and low-technology to meet individual, classroom, and teacher needs. Designs classroom activities for diverse-ability learners that integrate content-specific software; is acutely aware of the developmental appropriateness of selected software.

## High Degree of Competence

### Competent

Is able to use computer technology and software provided by C. T. or school. Is able to use high- and low-technology provided. Implements simple content-specific software; is aware of the need to determine appropriateness.

## Low Degree of Competence

### Unsatisfactory

Demonstrates little or no ability to employ computer technology. Demonstrates little or no ability to use high- and low-technology. Does not implement content-specific software and is unable to determine appropriateness.

|  | U | CO | O |
|---|---|---|---|
| MIDTERM EVALUATION............................ | | | |
| FINAL EVALUATION .................................. | | | |

# Category 13. Use of Multicultural Gender Fair (MCGF) Strategies

Demonstrates sensitivity to family, community diversity, language, asexuality/sexual orientation, and cultural identity; infuses MCGF strategies into all professional interactions.

## Outstanding

Respects all students and others; recognizes importance of race, ethnic background, gender, age, class, religion, language, or exceptionality to the culture of the classroom or the community-at-large. Initiates communication with regard to different perspectives in a tactful and sensitive manner. Celebrates diversity; models fair and equitable treatment of others; is comfortable and functional in cross-cultural settings; encourages students to be fair and equitable to others, both in the classroom and in the community-at-large. Infuses MCGF elements into all lessons, activities, and classes appropriately.

## High Degree of Competence

### Competent

Understands that diversity is wider than only ethnic differences; respects most students and provides culturally responsive teaching and learning. Listens to others and identifies different perspectives. Accepts diversity; is fair and equitable to students and others. Infuses MCGF elements into selected lessons, activities, or classes appropriately.

## Low Degree of Competence

### Unsatisfactory

Does not demonstrate respect for students and/or cultural practices within the classroom community and in the community-at-large. Does not listen; is oblivious or denies other perspectives. Denies diversity; is not fair or equitable to students and others; is oblivious or resistant to different cultures. Lacks sufficient knowledge, skill, or commitment to infuse MCGF elements.

|  | U | CO | O |
|---|---|---|---|
| MIDTERM EVALUATION.......................... | | | |
| FINAL EVALUATION ................................ | | | |

# Category 14. Human Relations Skills

Implements sound human relations and communication skills in order to foster productive, positive learning communities.

## Outstanding

Reaches out to others and establishes productive, interactive relationships and rapport, even in challenging situations. Facilitates classroom harmony and respect, even in conflict situations. Promotes self-confidence in all students, even in challenging situations. Has a diverse growing repertoire of ways to develop pupil self-concept in place. Provides constant student encouragement and assistance throughout the class day.

## High Degree of Competence

### Competent

Is able to respond positively to overtures of others and establish rapport and productive relationships in routine situations. Recognizes importance of facilitating classroom harmony and respect. Works to promote self-confidence in most students in most situations. Demonstrates ability to promote pupil self-concept in routine situations. Is accessible for assistance during scheduled times.

## Low Degree of Competence

### Unsatisfactory

Is inhibited; has difficulty initiating and/or maintaining comfortable relationships and rapport. Is oblivious to a lack of classroom harmony and respect. Rarely promotes self-confidence in others. Attributes little apparent importance to self-concept. Is rarely accessible to assist students.

|  | U | CO | O |
|---|---|---|---|
| MIDTERM EVALUATION........................... | | | |
| FINAL EVALUATION .................................. | | | |

# Category 15. Professional Characteristics and Leadership

Exhibits high-quality characteristics in professional and personal demeanor; professional behavior exemplifies role awareness and ethical conduct; takes initiative, recognizes and functions in the role of leader, or as an integral part of the staff, and takes on the appropriate role at the required time.

## Outstanding

Consistently demonstrates drive, industrious work ethic, and enthusiasm. Learns from teaching experiences, insightful self-evaluation and reflection; demonstrates deeper insights into teaching. Elicits and values specific constructive criticism; implements feedback. Is consistently dependable and follows through without reminders. Verbalizes and evidences high ethical standards, flexibility, congeniality, and positive attitude, even in difficult situations. Demonstrates leadership skills and collegiality; appropriately directs staff with sensitivity; is able to distinguish when to be a leader and when to be a team member. Consistently demonstrates poise and self-confidence and a well-developed sense of humor. Is often sought outside the classroom as a confidant and advisor.

## High Degree of Competence

### Competent

Demonstrates drive and enthusiasm, poise, flexibility, self-confidence, congeniality, and positive attitude in routine circumstances. Learning from teaching experiences, self-evaluating accurately, and constructive criticism. Is usually dependable and follows through with occasional reminders. Verbalizes high ethical standards and works to evidence them. Accepts role of leader when necessary, with the support of C. T. Demonstrates well developed sense of humor. Is sought out by students in classroom settings.

## Low Degree of Competence

### Unsatisfactory

Demonstrates minimal drive and enthusiasm, lacks flexibility, and fails to learn from mistakes. Avoids or is unreceptive to constructive criticism and is unrealistic or inaccurate in self-evaluations, shifting blame to others; rarely implements feedback. Displays limited dependability and/or follow through, even with reminders. Demonstrates undeveloped or inappropriate sense of humor. Has difficulty verbalizing and evidencing high ethical standards or leadership responsibilities. Has difficulty appearing congenial and positive, poised or self-confident and is rarely sought out by students.

|  | U | CO | O |
|---|---|---|---|
| MIDTERM EVALUATION............................ | | | |
| FINAL EVALUATION .................................. | | | |

# Category 1:  Knowledge of Care-Giving and Skills Areas

**Understands the central concepts of nurturing and care-giving; understands ages and stages of early childhood; plans and prepares nutritious foods when appropriate**

U = Unsatisfactory; LC = Low Competence; C = Competence; HC = High Competence; O = Outstanding

| Demonstrated Characteristics | U | LC | C | HC | O |
|---|---|---|---|---|---|
| **A. Possesses a Broad Knowledge of All Content Areas** | Demonstrates inaccurate or incomplete content knowledge, shows little or no effort to expand knowledge | Demonstrates minimal knowledge; strives for basic content knowledge competence | Displays basic content knowledge; seeks out additional information | Demonstrates advanced content knowledge; seeks out additional information | Demonstrates extensive content knowledge, seeks out additional information |
| **B. Integrates Knowledge of Basic Human Growth and Development into Learning Goals** | Is unable to use human growth knowledge in the development of a lesson | Attempts to use human growth knowledge in the development of a lesson | Uses human growth knowledge to develop an effective lesson | Presents lessons that include human growth knowledge and strives to make them meaningful to students | Presents meaningful lessons based on human growth knowledge and continually reinforces them |
| **C. Demonstrates Nurturing and Care-giving Skills** | Is unable to recognize the physical and affective needs of the students | Able to recognize physical and affective needs but does little to meet the needs | Recognizes physical and affective needs and attempts to meet the needs | Anticipates physical and affective needs and meets them effectively with routine understanding | Anticipates physical and affective needs and meets them with empathy and individuality |
| **D. Demonstrates Knowledge of Food Preparation and Its Nutritional Value** | Uses unsafe preparation, displays ignorance or disdain for nutritional needs of students | Attempts to prepare nutritious foods in a safe manner | Prepares nutritious food using safe and hygienic procedures | Prepares nutritious food and is conscientious about safe and hygienic procedures | Plans and implements high-quality, nutritious activities regularly into the curriculum and is conscientious about carrying out safe and hygienic procedures |

# Category 2: Knowledge of Learners and Learning Process

**Understands how children learn and differ in their approaches to learning; provides learning opportunities and experiences that are meaningful and that support their development cognitively, socially, emotionally, physically, and culturally; understands learners as a group and as individuals**

U = Unsatisfactory; LC = Low Competence; C = Competence; HC = High Competence; O = Outstanding

| Demonstrated Characteristics | U | LC | C | HC | O |
|---|---|---|---|---|---|
| **A. Awareness of Individual Needs** | Demonstrates no interest, skills, or ability in ascertaining needs | Demonstrates minimal interest, skill, or ability in ascertaining pupils' needs | Demonstrates basic ability to ascertain some of the pupils' needs | Demonstrates frequent abilities to ascertain many of the pupils' needs | Is consistently able to ascertain all pupils' needs |
| **B. Provides Meaningful and Relevant Learning Experiences Based on Students' Social, Emotional, Physical, and Cultural Needs and Interests** | Develops and teaches lessons and activities that lack consideration of students' needs and interests | Occasionally develops and teaches lessons and activities that show consideration of some of the students' needs and interests | Develops and teaches lessons and activities with the group's needs considered | Develops and teaches lessons and activities with the group's needs considered and some of the individual's needs | Teaches lessons and activities with all students' needs and interests considered |
| **C. Provides Cognitively Challenging and Complex Experiences** | Develops lessons and activities that are taught without consideration of students' cognitive levels | Develops and teaches lessons and activities that occasionally show consideration of some of the students' cognitive levels | Plans challenging and complex lessons and activities that are developed for the group's cognitive needs and some individuals' cognitive needs | Plans challenging and complex lessons and activities, with extensions that are developed based on students' cognitive needs | Displays flexibility in planning and implementing complex and challenging experiences based on students' cognitive needs |
| **D. Applies Learning Theories** | Displays no application or inaccurate application of theories | Demonstrates minimal application of theories | Demonstrates basic application of theories | Displays frequent application of theories | Demonstrates consistent application of theories |
| **E. Facilitates Logical Thinking** | Lacks demonstrated ability to lead pupils toward logical thinking or decision making | Sometimes alerts pupils to importance of logical thinking and decision making | Consistently alerts pupils to importance of logical thinking and decision making | Is developing ability to implement logical thinking and decision making with pupils | Inspires pupils to think logically and reserve decisions until all evidence has been examined |

# Category 3: Instructional Planning

**Plans instruction with children's health and safety as priority; understands, develops, and implements curriculum based on knowledge of subject matter, students' interests, developmental levels, the community, state/district/accreditation standards, and curriculum goals**

U = Unsatisfactory; LC = Low Competence; C = Competence; HC = High Competence; O = Outstanding

| Demonstrated Characteristics | U | LC | C | HC | O |
|---|---|---|---|---|---|
| **A. Plans in Advance** | Demonstrates no short- or long-range planning | Demonstrates minimal short- or long-range planning | Demonstrates basic short- and long-range planning | Demonstrates well-developed short- and long-range planning | Demonstrates well-developed short- and long-range planning |
| **B. Prepares High-Quality Lesson Plans that Meet Standards** | Demonstrates unclear purpose, organization, detail, and lack of alignment with standards | Demonstrates sketchy purpose, organization, detail, and alignment with standards | Demonstrates clear purpose, organization, sufficient detail, and alignment with standards | Demonstrates clear purpose, organization, detail, flexibility, and alignment with standards | Demonstrates clear purpose, organization, detail, flexibility, and alignment with standards: provides for individuality |
| **C. Incorporates and Meets Deadlines** | Does not meet planning or preparation deadlines | Is inconsistent in meeting, planning, and preparation deadlines | Usually meets planning and preparation deadlines | Consistently meets planning and preparation deadlines | Consistently exceeds planning and preparation deadlines |
| **D. Demonstrates Independence and Initiative** | Totally relies on C. T. to plan | Needs frequent input from C. T. to plan | Plans many lessons independently | Usually plans independently; shares drafted plans with the C. T. for feedback | Consistently plans independently; shares drafted plans with C. T. for feedback |
| **E. Acquires and Organizes Materials** | Has difficulty acquiring and organizing materials | Needs assistance to acquire or organize materials | Is able to acquire and organize prepared materials | Sometimes supplements prepared materials and organizes well | Consistently supplements prepared materials and organizes well |
| **F. Plans and Provides for a Safe and Healthy Environment in All Activities** | Does not plan for health and safety factors; displays ignorance for health and safety issues | Attempts to plan for health and safety issues in some areas | Generally plans for health and safety issues | Is diligent about planning for health and safety issues | Is consistently diligent about planning and for health and safety issues and anticipates and preempts unsafe situations |

# Category 4:  Use of Instructional Strategies

**Understands and uses a variety of instructional strategies; adapts teaching, curriculum, and caregiving styles to the diverse needs of students; understands and uses an appropriate balance between indirect and direct instruction; recognizes and capitalizes on teachable moments**

U = Unsatisfactory; LC = Low Competence; C = Competence; HC = High Competence; O = Outstanding

| Demonstrated Characteristics | U | LC | C | HC | O |
|---|---|---|---|---|---|
| **A. Balances Indirect and Direct Instruction** | Is unable to present content in an effective manner | Strives to present content clearly | Presents content clearly: attempts to make content relevant to students | Attempts to deliver content in a manner that facilitates active learning | Delivers content in a manner that facilitates active learning |
| **B. Implements Learning Goals and Objectives** | Sets unclear or inappropriate goals and objectives | Works to use pre-established objectives when setting goals | Makes good use of objectives in accompanying materials when setting goals | Works to evaluate achievement based on course goals and objectives | Evaluates achievement based on course goals and objectives |
| **C. Uses Appropriate Introductory, Transitional, and Concluding Statements** | Uses transition statements that are inconsistent and ineffective | Uses transition statements that are usually consistent, but appear mechanical | Understands and attempts to use transition statements that are relevant to learning and move the lesson fluently | Understands and generally evidences use of fluent, relevant transition statements | Evidences use of fluent transition statements; makes transitions relevant to learning and to appear natural |
| **D. Provides for Student Participation and Response** | Does not plan for or effectively use pupil participation and response | Shows some effort to encourage participation and response | Attempts to elicit maximum participation and response | Works to encourage participation and response by all students | Constructs and manages an environment that provides for maximum student participation and response |
| **E. Paces Instruction** | Demonstrates ineffective pacing | Shows some effort to pace instruction effectively | Sometimes paces instruction effectively | Often paces instruction effectively | Consistently paces instruction effectively |
| **F. Responds to Student-Initiated Discoveries and/or Queries** | Often ignores students or responds inappropriately | Shows some effort to respond promptly and appropriately | Is sometimes prompt and always appropriate in responding to students | Is always prompt and appropriate in responding to students | Is always prompt and appropriate in responding to students: anticipates questions, discoveries, and needs |
| **G. Adapts Teaching/Care-giving Style to Pupil Needs** | Rarely adapts or relies on one teaching/care-giving style | Works to develop teaching/care-giving style(s) | Sometimes adjusts teaching/care-giving style to students' needs | Displays well-developed teaching/care-giving style; is working to adjust to student needs | Displays well-developed teaching/care-giving style; consistently adjusts to student needs |

# Category 5: Learning Environment

**Creates a safe and healthy learning environment that encourages positive social interaction, active engagement in learning and self-motivation; fosters independence through accessible materials and toys; demonstrates a positive, enthusiastic attitude toward learners and the task of teaching; able to recognize unsafe situations and act upon them in a timely fashion**

U = Unsatisfactory; LC = Low Competence; C = Competence; HC = High Competence; O = Outstanding

| Demonstrated Characteristics | U | LC | C | HC | O |
|---|---|---|---|---|---|
| **A. Implements a Psychologically Safe Environment** | Is unaware of psychologically safe strategies | Is aware and begins to attempt to employ psychologically safe strategies | Implements a psychologically safe, positive, and encouraging classroom | Displays and implements sensitivity to the psychological needs of students | Displays and implements sensitivity to the safe, psychological needs and encourages perspective taking by the students |
| **B. Implements a Sound Classroom Climate** | Is not yet able to implement a sound classroom climate | Recognizes elements of a sound classroom climate and is beginning to implement them | Maintains a positive classroom climate; experiences few instances of negativism | Maintains a consistently positive classroom climate | Facilitates students' desire to maintain a sound classroom climate |
| **C. Fosters Independence** | Makes no effort to make materials and toys accessible | Makes a few toys accessible; requires children to ask for most materials and toys | Makes an adequate number of materials and toys accessible for use and clean-up by children | Makes a variety of materials and toys accessible for use and clean-up by children; supplies toys and materials if children request them | Makes a variety of materials and toys accessible for use and clean-up by children; supplies toys and materials in anticipation of students' needs; encourages children to choose toys and materials and develops new materials for their use |
| **D. Displays a Positive Attitude toward the Children and the Task of Teaching** | Displays a negative attitude about teaching and children | Displays pleasure toward children or teaching | Displays pleasure in the children and teaching | Displays pleasure in teaching and the children, and the children can recognize it | Displays enthusiasm and positive attitude in all aspects of teaching, even in stressful situations; facilitates students' desire to maintain a positive climate |

# Category 6:  Classroom Management

**Creates a fair, respectful, positive environment; sets clear expectations and reasonable consequences; uses both direct and indirect guidance techniques to encourage appropriate, positive personal behavior choices; honors children's choices when appropriate; able to treat each child with dignity and as an individual**

U = Unsatisfactory; LC = Low Competence; C = Competence; HC = High Competence; O = Outstanding

| Demonstrated Characteristics | U | LC | C | HC | O |
|---|---|---|---|---|---|
| **A. Plans for Procedures and Management** | Demonstrates little or no procedural management | Is working to learn basic classroom and school procedures | Seeks help in planning some specific classroom procedures | Seeks help in planning non-routine classroom procedures | Has learned to manage routine procedure; is able to adjust for non-routine needs |
| **B. Implements Diverse Classroom Management Strategies** | Is unable to maintain adequate classroom management | Is beginning to work toward effective management strategies | Is sometimes able to apply effective classroom management | Usually maintains effective classroom management using diverse strategies | Consistently implements classroom management techniques to stimulate learning environment |
| **C. Handles Guidance Problems** | Is unsuccessful in resolving guidance problems | Is beginning to recognize when appropriate guidance techniques are needed | Implements appropriate guidance techniques that produce desired results | Recognizes emerging guidance problems and implements effective, appropriate guidance techniques | Anticipates guidance problems; preventively implements effective, appropriate guidance techniques |
| **D. Establishes Expectations and Holds Students Accountable** | Rarely establishes expectations or holds students accountable | Recognizes the need for expectations and holds students accountable only with C. T.'s help | Sets standards and strives to consistently hold students accountable for their work and behavior | Is consistent and clear in establishing expectations and holding students accountable for their work and behavior | Is consistent and clear in establishing and monitoring expectations and student accountability |
| **E. Implements Fairness and Equity** | Shows bias or uses statements that result in unfairness | Recognizes need to be unbiased | Takes an unbiased approach to classroom interactions | Effectively models fairness and equity and is beginning to develop awareness of student bias in classroom interactions | Effectively models fairness and equity and encourages students to exhibit fairness and equity in classroom |

| Demonstrated Characteristics | U | LC | C | HC | O |
|---|---|---|---|---|---|
| **F. Offers Opportunities for Decision Making** | Makes all decisions for students | Provides some opportunities for decision making | Provides opportunities for students to choose desired behaviors and activities | Provides opportunities for student choice and honors most decisions | Anticipates and provides opportunities for student choice; honors the appropriate decisions and renegotiates the inappropriate ones |

# Category 7: Use of Communication Strategies

**Uses knowledge of both oral and non-verbal communication techniques to foster active inquiry, collaboration, and supportive interactions that are developmentally appropriate**

U = Unsatisfactory; LC = Low Competence; C = Competence; HC = High Competence; O = Outstanding

| Demonstrated Characteristics | U | LC | C | HC | O |
|---|---|---|---|---|---|
| **A. Oral Communication Skills** | Uses a weak, monotonous, or unexpressive voice | Works to develop oral communication skills | Uses a pleasant, well-modulated voice with adequate projection | Works to effectively vary vocal cues, rate, volume, and enunciation | Effectively varies vocal cues, rate, volume, and enunciation |
| **B. Written Communication Skills** | Is disorganized or displays problems with spelling, grammar, or mechanics | Works toward basic competence in organization, spelling, grammar, and/or mechanics | Is organized; proofs carefully to correct most spelling, grammar, and mechanics | Is organized; is accurate with spelling, grammar, and mechanics | Is organized; uses excellent spelling, grammar, mechanics, and overall style |
| **C. Non-verbal Communication Skills** | Uses negative, conflicting, or distracting non-verbal communication or mannerisms | Works toward basic competence in non-verbal communication | Shows basic competence in non-verbal communication that supports verbal cues | Builds on basic non-verbal competence to elicit natural, reciprocal communication | Uses non-verbal communication; elicits natural, reciprocal communication |
| **D. Standard English Proficiency** | Makes frequent errors, grammatical mistakes, or uses inappropriate language for school setting | Works toward basic competence in standard English proficiency | Demonstrates basic competence in standard English | Builds on standard English basics to be fluent, clear, expressive | Demonstrates mastery of standard English: is fluent, clear, expressive |
| **E. Interpersonal Communication with Students** | Lacks clarity in making explanations, fails to communicate effectively with students | Works toward basic competency in communicating with students | Usually communicates effectively with students | Communicates effectively with students; is working toward depth and subtlety | Models depth and subtlety in interpersonal communication with students |
| **F. Language of Subject Matter** | Uses language of subject matter incorrectly and seems unaware when students do so | Works toward basic competency in using and encouraging language of subject matter | Encourages appropriate usage of subject matter language | Encourages appropriate usage of subject matter language and strives to be a good model | Consistently models and teaches appropriate usage of subject matter language |
| **G. Implements Varied Questioning Techniques** | Does not demonstrate varied, basic questioning techniques | Works to demonstrate varied, basic questioning techniques | Demonstrates varied, basic questioning techniques | Is beginning to demonstrate varied, advanced questioning techniques | Consistently demonstrates varied, advanced questioning techniques |

# Category 8: Use of Assessing/Diagnosing/Evaluating Strategies

**Understands and uses a variety of formal, informal, and authentic assessment strategies that align with instructional approaches; takes actions to determine what strengths and problems exist and responds appropriately to the assessment results; evaluates in an objective manner**

U = Unsatisfactory; LC = Low Competence; C = Competence; HC = High Competence; O = Outstanding

| Demonstrated Characteristics | U | LC | C | HC | O |
|---|---|---|---|---|---|
| **A. Develops Variety of Assessment Materials** | Is unable to develop appropriate assessments or utilize pre-existing assessments effectively | Depends on pre-existing assessments exclusively | Works to get beyond pre-existing formal assessments; uses assessments objectively | Works to develop both informal and formal progress assessments that set the stage for re-teaching and individual remediation | Develops authentic progress assessments that set the stage for re-teaching and individual remediation |
| **B. Assesses and Responds to Formative and Summative Assessments** | Bases evaluation on traditional criteria with little or no understanding of the limitations of these procedures | Works to assess formative understanding prior to summative assessments; uses traditional assessments methods only | Provides adequate activities to assess formative understanding and monitors pupil progress; plans additional teaching based on assessment results | Works to assess understanding and accurately monitors progress; provides individual as well as group assistance based on assessment results | Assesses understanding accurately; consistently responds to results by providing individual and group assistance and seeks out other resources |
| **C. Communicates Progress** | Is often unclear, ineffective, or inconsistent in communicating progress to students and parents | Works to be clear and consistent in communicating progress to parents | Is usually clear and consistent in communicating progress to parents in an informal setting | Is clear and consistent in communicating progress to parents in an informal setting; is working on formal settings | Is clear and consistent in communicating progress to parents in both formal and informal settings |
| **D. Keeps Records** | Does not maintain adequate records | Attempts to maintain adequate records | Usually maintains adequate records | Consistently maintains needed records | Consistently maintains needed records; designs flexible systems as needed |

# Category 9:  Use of Motivational Strategies

**Uses multiple techniques, materials, and settings to kindle and sustain interest of learners; motivates by personal behavior; able to identify interest and non-interest behaviors and respects them**

U = Unsatisfactory; LC = Low Competence; C = Competence; HC = High Competence; O = Outstanding

| Demonstrated Characteristics | U | LC | C | HC | O |
|---|---|---|---|---|---|
| **A. Involves Students in Classroom Activities in a Stimulating Environment** | Has difficulty establishing a stimulating environment | Sometimes establishes a stimulating environment | Often establishes a stimulating environment in typical circumstances | Uses a variety of motivational strategies; works to establish a stimulating environment even in challenging circumstances | Consistently establishes a stimulating environment, even in challenging circumstances |
| **B. Provides Motivational Activities** | Uses unimaginative or inappropriate motivational activities; shows little or no enthusiasm for teaching or students | Uses a limited repertoire of strategies regardless of student motivation; shows contrived enthusiasm for teaching and for learners | Integrates motivational activities and personal enthusiasm into standard curricular materials | Works to integrate diverse motivational activities from a variety of sources; participates in activities with genuine enthusiasm | Consistently kindles students' interest by a variety of motivational strategies; uses challenging circumstances to enhance learning; participates in activities with genuine enthusiasm |
| **C. Recognizes Pupil Motivational Level** | Underestimates importance of motivation and forces participation | Underestimates importance of motivation and allows disinterested students to disengage | Displays accurate recognition of student motivational levels; works to motivate students in activities | Demonstrates a proactive influence on motivation; is gaining awareness on how to modify during lessons and activities; is aware of the teachable moment | Displays a proactive influence on motivation; recognizes and uses student motivations to plan before, during, and after lessons to better reach the students at their levels; uses the teachable moment effectively |
| **D. Maintains Pupil Interest** | Shows inadequacy in maintaining pupil interest; struggles with discipline problems that result | Works to maintain pupil interest and decrease discipline problems in routine circumstances | Maintains pupil interest; experiences few discipline problems in routine circumstances | Works to maintain pupil interest; experiences few discipline problems, even in challenging circumstances | Maintains pupil interest; experiences few discipline problems, even in challenging circumstances |

# Category 10:  Use of Problem-Solving/Decision-Making Strategies

**Reflects on teaching during and after lessons in order to recognize and solve problems and make decisions; examines situations from various perspectives and is appropriately decisive; able to seek out information from others and other sources to solve instructional or behavioral problems**

U = Unsatisfactory; LC = Low Competence; C = Competence; HC = High Competence; O = Outstanding

| Demonstrated Characteristics | U | LC | C | HC | O |
|---|---|---|---|---|---|
| **A. Reflects Formatively and Summatively** | Is unable to reflect during or after lessons | Shows reflection skills after lessons but not during | Is able to reflect on obvious issues or concerns regarding his/her teaching | Is able to reflect accurately, sensitively, and thoroughly about his/her teaching in most situations | Consistently reflects accurately, sensitively, and thoroughly about his/her teaching |
| **B. Recognizes Problems and Arrives at Decisions** | Demonstrates little independent thinking or strength of own opinion in problem finding and problem solving; relies on C. T. for decisions | Works to develop independent thinking and problem finding/solving skills; relies on C. T. for decisions | Is developing independent thinking and problem-finding/solving skills; makes decisions through discussion with C. T. | Has independent thinking and problem-finding/solving skills in place; identifies students' needs and provides resources to aid in making joint decisions with C. T. | Displays advanced independent thinking and problem-finding/solving skills; thoroughly examines needs and resources available and shares decisions/rationale with C. T. if necessary |
| **C. Demonstrates Open-Mindedness** | Is reluctant to consider viewpoints of others before making final decisions | Is occasionally willing to consider viewpoints of others before making final decisions | Often considers viewpoints of others before making final decisions | Is beginning to welcome viewpoints of others and knows when to elicit them; considers them before making final decisions | Welcomes viewpoints of others, knows when to elicit them and considers them before making final decisions |
| **D. Follows up on Decisions** | Is overly dependent; relies on others to follow up on decisions; is unwilling to follow up | Works to become self-reliant in collecting and organizing materials to support decisions | Collects and organizes materials to support decisions | Works to fit materials and actions to situations and communicates decisions to others involved | Easily fits materials and actions to situations, communicates decisions to others involved, and follows up independently |
| **E. Employs Research-oriented Approaches to Problems** | Is reluctant to investigate or seek solutions to problems | Is beginning to question merits of various solutions to problems | Raises questions about the merit of various solutions to problems and may attempt to research alternatives | Questions merits of various solutions; is beginning to seek alternatives to solve instructional problems or find answers to educational questions | Consistently raises questions and actively researches alternatives to solve instructional problems or to find answers to educational questions |

# Category 11: Home-School-Community Relations

## Fosters relationships with colleagues, parents, and, as needed, agencies in the larger community

U = Unsatisfactory; LC = Low Competence; C = Competence; HC = High Competence; O = Outstanding

| Demonstrated Characteristics | U | LC | C | HC | O |
|---|---|---|---|---|---|
| **A. Initiates Contacts with Parents/ Guardians** | Fails to see value of contact or avoids family contact | Works to be comfortable contacting parents/guardians about general information, avoids specific information about the child | Regularly contacts parents/guardians on class or individual basis | Works to involve parents/guardians in ongoing school activities and student progress | Actively involves parents/guardians as part of child's total educational experience |
| **B. Understands and Demonstrates Conferencing Skills** | Sees no value in communicating with parents/ guardians; unwilling to participate in conferences with C. T. | Understands the importance of conferencing skills, but only observes conferences that are led by C. T. | Understands conferencing skills; supports the C.T. with information during conferences | Understands conferencing skills and assists the C.T. in conferences | Understands the value of accurate, continual communication with parents/ guardians; able to lead a conference and demonstrates the ability to be tactfully honest |
| **C. Works with Colleagues** | Avoids working with colleagues | Works with colleagues only when absolutely necessary | Is able to work with colleagues on a routine basis | Takes initiative to become involved and part of the school team | Has become an integral part of the school staff by sharing information and responsibilities |
| **D. Works with Community Resources (as Needed)** | Avoids contact with community resources | Contacts resources only when suggested and initiated by C.T. | Works with C.T. to involve community resources | Takes initiative in contacting community resources | Takes initiative for contact and follow-up with community resources |

# Category 12:  Use of Technology

**Integrates the computer and other high- and low-technology into teacher preparation, classroom teaching activities, assessment, and/or documentation**

U = Unsatisfactory; LC = Low Competence; C = Competence; HC = High Competence; O = Outstanding

| Demonstrated Characteristics | U | LC | C | HC | O |
|---|---|---|---|---|---|
| **A. Employs Computer Technology in Teaching and Preparation** | Demonstrates little or no ability to employ computer technology | Works to improve limited ability to employ computer technology | Is able to use computer technology and software provided by C. T. or school | Works to locate software to meet individual, class, or teacher needs | Is proficient in location of software to meet individual, class, and teacher needs |
| **B. Employs High- and Low-Technology** | Demonstrates little or no ability to use high- and low-technology | Works to improve limited ability to employ high- and low-technology | Is able to use high- and low-technology provided | Works to locate high- and low-technology to meet individual, classroom, and teacher needs | Is proficient in locating high- and low-technology to meet individual, classroom, and teacher needs |
| **C. Uses Instructional Software** | Does not implement content-specific software and is unable to determine appropriateness | Indicates awareness of content-specific software; is unaware of appropriateness of software | Implements simple content-specific software; is aware of the need to determine appropriateness | Designs classroom activities to integrate content-specific software that is developmentally appropriate | Designs classroom activities for diverse-ability learners that integrate content-specific software; is acutely aware of the developmental appropriateness of selected software |

# Category 13: Use of Multicultural Gender Fair (MCGF) Strategies

**Demonstrates sensitivity to family, community diversity, and cultural identity; infuses MCGF strategies into all professional interactions**

U = Unsatisfactory; LC = Low Competence; C = Competence; HC = High Competence; O = Outstanding

| Demonstrated Characteristics | U | LC | C | HC | O |
|---|---|---|---|---|---|
| **A. Recognizes Multifaceted Cultural Identity** | Does not demonstrate respect for students and/or cultural practices within the classroom community and in the community-at-large | Demonstrates selective respect for students; begins to recognize the importance of the culture of the classroom or the community-at-large | Understands that diversity is wider than only ethnic differences; respects most students and provides culturally responsive teaching and learning | Respects all students; works to recognize the importance of race, ethnic background, gender, age, class, religion, language, or exceptionality to the culture of the classroom or the community-at-large | Respects all students and others; recognizes importance of race, ethnic background, gender, age, class, religion, language, or exceptionality to the culture of the classroom or the community-at-large |
| **B. Infuses MCGF Elements** | Lacks sufficient knowledge, skill, or commitment to infuse MCGF elements | Works to improve insufficient knowledge and skills to infuse MCGF elements | Infuses MCGF elements into selected lessons, activities, or classes appropriately | Infuses MCGF elements into most lessons, activities, and classes appropriately | Infuses MCGF elements into all lessons, activities, and classes appropriately |
| **C. Responds to Diversity** | Denies diversity; is not fair or equitable to students and others; is oblivious or resistant to different cultures | Tolerates diversity; is beginning to appreciate differences | Accepts diversity; is fair and equitable to students and others | Values diversity; models being fair and equitable to students; seeks cross-cultural experiences as a learner | Celebrates diversity; models fair and equitable treatment of others; is comfortable and functional in cross-cultural settings; encourages students to be fair and equitable to others, both in the classroom and in the community-at-large |
| **D. Listens and Is Perceptive with Regard to Perspectives of Students, Parents, and Others** | Does not listen; is oblivious or denies other perspectives | Is beginning to listen to other perspectives | Listens to others and identifies different perspectives | Listens and responds to different perspectives with sensitivity | Initiates communication with regard to different perspectives in a tactful and sensitive manner |

# Category 14: Human Relations Skills

**Implements sound human relations and communication skills in order to foster productive, positive learning communities**

U = Unsatisfactory; LC = Low Competence; C = Competence; HC = High Competence; O = Outstanding

| Demonstrated Characteristics | U | LC | C | HC | O |
|---|---|---|---|---|---|
| **A. Promotes Self-confidence in Others** | Rarely promotes self-confidence in others | Works to promote self-confidence in some students in some situations | Works to promote self-confidence in most students in most situations | Regularly promotes self-confidence in most students, except in challenging situations | Promotes self-confidence in all students, even in challenging situations |
| **B. Establishes Relationships and Rapport** | Is inhibited; has difficulty initiating and/or maintaining comfortable relationships and rapport | Works to respond positively to overtures of others, attempts to establish productive relationships and rapport in routine situations | Is able to respond positively to overtures of others and establish rapport and productive relationships in routine situations | Reaches out to others to establish productive, interactive relationships and rapport | Reaches out to others and establishes productive, interactive relationships and rapport, even in challenging situations |
| **C. Provides Student Assistance** | Is rarely accessible to assist students | Is working to be accessible for student assistance | Is accessible for assistance during scheduled times | Is working to provide constant student encouragement and assistance throughout the class day | Provides constant student encouragement and assistance throughout the class day |
| **D. Promotes Classroom Harmony and Respect** | Is oblivious to a lack of classroom harmony and respect | Is beginning to recognize importance of facilitating classroom harmony and respect | Recognizes importance of facilitating classroom harmony and respect | Facilitates classroom harmony and respect in most situations | Facilitates classroom harmony and respect, even in conflict situations |
| **E. Demonstrates Ability to Build Student Self-Concepts** | Attributes little apparent importance to self-concept | Is working to demonstrate ability to promote pupil self-concept in routine situations | Demonstrates ability to promote pupil self-concept in routine situations | Is working to develop a diverse, growing repertoire of ways to develop pupil self-concept | Has a diverse growing repertoire of ways to develop pupil self-concept in place |

# Category 15: Professional Characteristics and Leadership

**Exhibits high-quality characteristics in professional and personal demeanor; professional behavior exemplifies role awareness and ethical conduct; takes initiative, recognizes and functions in the role of leader, or as an integral part of the staff, and takes on the appropriate role at the required time**

U = Unsatisfactory; LC = Low Competence; C = Competence; HC = High Competence; O = Outstanding

| Demonstrated Characteristics | U | LC | C | HC | O |
|---|---|---|---|---|---|
| **A. Approaches Teaching Proactively** | Demonstrates minimal drive and enthusiasm | Is beginning to demonstrate drive and enthusiasm | Demonstrates drive and enthusiasm | Strives to demonstrate drive, industrious work ethic, and enthusiasm | Consistently demonstrates drive, industrious work ethic, and enthusiasm |
| **B. Learns from Experience** | Repeats mistakes; evidences difficulty with experience-based learning | Is occasionally able to learn from experience when experience is dramatic | Is able to learn from teaching experiences | Learns from teaching experiences, demonstrates some insights into teaching | Learns from teaching experiences, demonstrates deeper insights into teaching |
| **C. Responds to Constructive Criticism and Feedback** | Avoids or is unreceptive to constructive criticism; shifts blame; rarely implements feedback | Is beginning to accept constructive criticism; still offers excuses; sometimes implements feedback | Accepts constructive criticism; implements feedback | Is beginning to elicit constructive criticism; implements feedback | Elicits specific constructive criticism; implements feedback |
| **D. Demonstrates Dependability** | Displays limited dependability and/or follow-through, even with reminders | Is working to be responsible and follows through, with reminders | Is usually dependable and follows through, with occasional reminders | Is working to be dependable and follows through without reminders | Is consistently dependable and follows through without reminders |
| **E. Demonstrates Ethical Conduct** | Demonstrates difficulty verbalizing and evidencing high ethical standards | Verbalizes high ethical standards but rarely evidences them | Verbalizes high ethical standards and works to evidence them | Verbalizes and evidences high ethical standards in routine circumstances | Verbalizes and evidences high ethical standards, even in difficult situations |
| **F. Projects a Positive Demeanor** | Has difficulty appearing congenial and positive | Attempts to be congenial and positive in routine circumstances | Is usually congenial and positive in routine circumstances | Is working to be congenial and positive, even in stressful circumstances | Is consistently congenial and positive, even in stressful circumstances |

| Demonstrated Characteristics | U | LC | C | HC | O |
|---|---|---|---|---|---|
| **G. Displays Leadership with Staff** | Is unaware of and/or avoids all leadership responsibilities | Is aware of the need for leadership but hesitates to take responsibility without extensive support from the C. T. | Accepts role of leader when necessary, with the support of C. T. | Is able to demonstrate leadership skills most of the time; relies on C. T. in stressful circumstances | Demonstrates leadership skills and collegiality; appropriately directs staff with sensitivity; is able to distinguish when to be a leader and when to be a team member |
| **H. Demonstrates a Sense of Humor** | Demonstrates undeveloped or inappropriate sense of humor | Is working to develop appropriate sense of humor | Demonstrates well developed sense of humor | Displays well developed sense of humor; works to implement humor in classroom interactions | Demonstrates well developed sense of humor; implements it appropriately in daily practice |
| **I. Demonstrates Poise and Self-confidence** | Demonstrates lack of poise and self-confidence even in routine situations | Is working to demonstrate poise and self-confidence in routine situations | Demonstrates poise and self-confidence in routine situations | Is working to demonstrate poise and self-confidence in routine and stressful situations | Consistently demonstrates poise and self-confidence in routine and stressful situations |
| **J. Demonstrates Flexibility** | Has difficulty demonstrating flexibility, even in routine situation | Is working to demonstrate flexibility in routine situations | Demonstrates flexibility in routine situations | Is working to demonstrate flexibility in routine or new situations | Demonstrates flexibility in routine or new situations |
| **K. Demonstrates Approachability** | Is rarely sought out by students in classroom settings | Is beginning to be sought out by students in classroom settings | Is sought out by students in classroom settings | Is beginning to be sought out as a confidant and classroom advisor | Is often sought outside the classroom as a confidant and advisor |
| **L. Demonstrates Ability to Self-evaluate** | Is unrealistic or inaccurate in self-evaluations | Is sometimes able to self-evaluate accurately | Is usually able to self-evaluate accurately | Is working toward insightful evaluation of self-performance | Demonstrates insightful evaluation of self-performance |

# I. Final Evaluation Procedures For Early Childhood Student Teachers

The preparation of the final evaluation is an important responsibility. Time and careful thought should be given to this document. The final evaluation may become a part of the official credentials for prospective teachers. The university coordinator of student teaching and/or supervisor will provide instruction on how the final evaluation form is to be completed. There will be a final conference for the purpose of discussing the evaluation with the student teacher. The university coordinator, via the Office of Student Field Experiences, will assume final responsibility for submission of the student teaching evaluation materials to the student teacher's university record.

In evaluating a student teacher, the cooperating teachers are asked to indicate on the fifteen-point checklist the student's level of performance as U (unsatisfactory), LC (low competent), CO (competent), HC (high competent), or O (outstanding). Note: When evaluating, the cooperating teacher should think of their student teacher in terms of other teacher candidates at the completion of their student teaching experience. It is necessary to avoid comparing the student teacher to experienced teachers. While some are capable of teaching at a demonstrated level of master teacher, most will lack that level of experience.

## Writing the Narrative Section

The following guidelines are to assist you in preparing a narrative description of the student teacher's experience. As the narrative is written, consider the following ideas:

1. The performance rankings should be consistent with and supported by the written narrative.

2. The narrative should contain objective statements that are supported by specific descriptions. For example:

   *"Ms. Andrews effectively guided the pupils' learning of important concepts in content material. She carefully identified and taught the necessary vocabulary and prepared study guides which were used to stimulate discussion."*

3. Narrative statements are precise, descriptive, and should never be open to misinterpretation. The majority of the narrative should be written in *past tense* since the final evaluation comes at the end of the student teaching experience. *Future tense* should be used when making predictions of the student teacher's future potential as a classroom teacher.

The written evaluation should address the following areas but doesn't necessarily need to be in the suggested six-paragraph format. It is common to find written evaluations covering the same information in four or five paragraphs.

**Paragraph one—classroom setting**. This paragraph describes the environment. Information about the community and the school, the range of student abilities, the socio-economic background of the pupils, the setting in which the student teacher worked including the number of pupils, classes, or subject matter, a description of the teaching responsibilities and extra duties may be included in this paragraph.

**Paragraph two—special skills and competencies**. Describe special skills that the student teacher possessed and demonstrated. For example: lesson planning, evaluating students' work, planning and carrying out worthwhile activities, incorporating a variety of learning styles into lessons, constructing bulletin boards and/or learning centers, etc. Anything that was done especially well should be emphasized.

**Paragraph three—classroom management**. Describe the student teacher's ability to establish rapport with pupils and how effective were her/his classroom management skills.

**Paragraph four—areas needing improvement**. *(Optional)* Describe any weaknesses that the student teacher possesses. Also reflect on the student teacher's ability to correct said weak areas and offer a prediction of the success of the student teacher in achieving correction of the same.

**Paragraph five—character and personality**. Describe any professional characteristic(s) that might make this student a good beginning teacher (reflective, personable, dedicated, responsible, hard working, conscientious, energetic, intelligent, open to constructive feedback, ebullient, maintains a professional appearance, etc.). Discuss how the student teacher related to you, the cooperating teacher; administration; staff; and parents.

**Paragraph six—prediction for success**. Give a professional opinion as to the probable success of this student teacher based on personal growth and professional development shown throughout the student teaching experience.

The length of the final narrative should be approximately 400–500 words. However, if more is necessary to capture the true flavor of the student teacher, then more narrative should be written. *Note: Final evaluation forms can also be attained at* <u>*http://www.uni.edu/coe/departments/office-student-field-experiences/ information-faculty/supervisors*</u>.

**FINAL EVALUATION**
**OF**
**EARLY CHILDHOOD STUDENT TEACHING**

Name: _____

| Last | First | Middle/Maiden |
|------|-------|---------------|

_____

| Student ID Number | Major |
|-------------------|-------|

_____

| Grade Level(s) | Building(s) | School District |
|----------------|-------------|-----------------|

_____

| City | State | Zip Code |
|------|-------|----------|

_____

| University Coordinator | Clinical Supervisor | Cooperating Teacher |
|------------------------|---------------------|---------------------|

Office _____     _____     Building _____

Phone     Area          Beginning and Ending Dates     Phone     Area

Evaluation Scale: U...Unsatisfactory; CO...Competent; HC...Highly Competent; O...Outstanding        Check the Appropriate Circle

**COMPETENCIES/CHARACTERISTICS**        **PERFORMANCE LEVELS**

| | | U | LC | CO | HC | O |
|--|--|---|----|----|----|---|
| 1. | **Knowledge of Care-Giving and Skills Areas** <br> Understands the central concepts of nurturing and care-giving; understands ages and stages of early childhood; plans and prepares nutritious foods when appropriate. | O | O | O | O | O |
| 2. | **Knowledge of Learners and Learning Process** <br> Understands how children learn and differ in their approaches to learning; provides learning opportunities and experiences that are meaningful and that support their development cognitively, socially, emotionally, physically and culturally; understands learners as a group and as individuals. | O | O | O | O | O |
| 3. | **Instructional Planning** <br> Plans instruction with children's health and safety as priority; understands, develops and implements curriculum based on knowledge of subject matter, students' interests, developmental levels, the community, state/district/accreditation standards, and curriculum goals. | O | O | O | O | O |
| 4. | **Use of Instructional Strategies** <br> Understands and uses a variety of instructional strategies; adapts teaching, curriculum, and care-giving styles to the diverse needs of students; understands and uses an appropriate balance between indirect and direct instruction; recognizes and capitalizes on teachable moments. | O | O | O | O | O |
| 5. | **Learning Environment** <br> Creates a safe and healthy learning environment that encourages positive social interaction, active engagement in learning and self-motivation; fosters independence through accessible materials and toys; demonstrates a positive, enthusiastic attitude toward learners and the task of teaching; able to recognize unsafe situations and act upon them in a timely fashion. | O | O | O | O | O |
| 6. | **Classroom Management** · <br> Creates a fair, respectful, positive environment; sets clear expectations and reasonable consequences; uses both direct and indirect guidance techniques to encourage appropriate positive personal behavior choices; honors children's choices when appropriate; able to treat each child with dignity and as an individual. | O | O | O | O | O |
| 7. | **Use of Communication Strategies** <br> Uses knowledge of both oral, and non-verbal communication techniques to foster active inquiry, collaboration and supportive interactions that are developmentally appropriate. | O | O | O | O | O |
| 8. | **Use of Assessing/Diagnosing/Evaluating Strategies** <br> Understands and uses a variety of formal, informal, and authentic assessment strategies that align with instructional approaches; takes actions to determine what strengths and problems exist and responds appropriately to the assessment results; evaluates in an objective manner. | O | O | O | O | O |
| 9. | **Use of Motivational Strategies** <br> Uses multiple techniques, materials, and settings to kindle and sustain interest of learners; motivates by personal behavior; able to identify interest and non-interest behaviors and respects them. | O | O | O | O | O |
| 10. | **Use of Problem-Solving/Decision Making Strategies** <br> Reflects on teaching during and after lessons in order to recognize and solve problems and make decisions; examines situations from various perspectives and is appropriately decisive; able to seek out information from others and other sources to solve instructional or behavioral problems. | O | O | O | O | O |
| 11. | **Home-School-Community Relations** <br> Fosters relationships with colleagues, parents, and, as needed, agencies in the larger community. | O | O | O | O | O |
| 12. | **Use of Technology** <br> Integrates the computer and other high- and low-technology into preparation, classroom teaching activites, assessment and/or documentation. | O | O | O | O | O |
| 13. | **Use of Multicultural Gender Fair (MCGF) Strategies** <br> Demonstrates sensitivity to family, community diversity and cultural identity; infuses MCGF strategies into all professional interactions. | O | O | O | O | O |
| 14. | **Human Relations Skills** <br> Implements sound human relations and communication skills in order to foster productive, positive learning communities. | O | O | O | O | O |
| 15. | **Professional Characteristics and Leadership** <br> Exhibits high quality characteristics in professional and personal demeanor; professional behavior exemplifies role awareness and ethical conduct; takes initiative, recognizes and functions in the role of leader, or as an integral part of the staff, and takes on the appropriate role at the required time. | O | O | O | O | O |

# Some Evaluative Qualities of Student Teachers

Use these suggested qualities as guides when writing your narrative portion of the student teacher final evaluation.

Organizational ability
Cooperation with professional staff
Ability to establish rapport with staff
Classroom management
Ability to write good lesson plans
Ability to relate content to students
Responses to suggestions
Utilization of media/technology
Creativity
Adaptability
Speech: speed, tone, volume, language usage
Understanding of students
Sense of humor
Questioning skills
Appearance
Enthusiasm
Ability to motivate students
Well rounded background
Ability to develop and use objectives
Recognizes individual differences
Pacing of class activity
Ability to anticipate problem areas
Ability to evaluate self
Strong professional ethics
Correct pronunciation of names
Respect for difference
Mediating conflict
Confidence
Tact
Empathy
Promptness
Initiative
Cultural awareness
Technological skills
Computer literacy
Conceptualization
Facilitates home/school relations
Awareness of service learning
Integrity
Responsibility
Professional relations

Dependability
Motivated
Positive role model

# Frequently Asked Questions (FAQ's) and Forms

"Don't worry about failures, worry about the changes you miss when you don't even try."
—*Jack Canfield*

# A. Frequently Asked Questions Related to Supervising a Student Teacher

1. **How quickly should the student teacher be worked into teaching?**

   The student teaching experience is intended for student teachers to obtain actual teaching experience in the field. The more opportunities they have to teach and work in their field placement, the more rewarding is the experience. Thus, student teachers should be assigned some initial responsibilities, gradually working up to the point to where they assume the full teaching duties for the cooperating teacher. Full responsibilities normally occur in the fourth through eighth week of the student teaching experience, depending on the readiness of the student teacher.

2. **For what length of time should the student teacher assume all or most of the teaching responsibility?**

   It is suggested that student teachers assume full responsibility for the classroom for a minimum of two weeks with their lesson plans. It is important that students do not feel overwhelmed initially by classroom duties. As a result, it is suggested that the takeover of instructional responsibilities be a gradual process, resulting in greater initiative on the student teacher's part.

3. **Is the student teacher required to turn in lesson plans?**

   All teaching should be based on some previously planned, written objectives. Lesson plans are considered to be a "given." Student teachers need not turn in their lesson plans to the university coordinator or supervisor, but, at times, they may request to review them. Lesson plan design and functionality is the responsibility of the cooperating teacher. Student teachers should conform to their requirements.

   As to the format, the cooperating teacher may wish to have the student teacher follow the same format she/he follows.

4. **Should the student teacher be required to teach a unit?**

   The student teaching experience is more satisfying when the student teacher can see the beginning and ending of a series of related lessons. Teaching a unit can meet this need. Developing, planning, and teaching a unit is recommended if circumstances make this feasible.

5. **Do UNI student teachers receive a letter grade for student teaching?**

   Student teachers do not receive a letter grade. The final evaluation papers, placed with the student teacher's professional credentials, are considered to be the "grade." Student teachers receive a "credit" or "no credit" mark on their transcript.

6. **Is it necessary that the student teacher attend the seminar?**

   The seminars are considered to be an integral part of the student teaching experience. They are devoted to such themes as teaching techniques, lesson design, classroom management, resumes, the interview process, etc. The seminars equate to teacher in-service. For this reason, student teachers are required to attend these professional growth experiences.

7. **Can the cooperating teacher require certain activities of the student teacher?**

As a specialist, you may have some activities planned that would greatly add to the overall experience of the student teacher's time with you. In the past, cooperating teachers have asked student teachers to organize field trips, start activity files, keep a diary of experiences, visit with parents, help with bus duties, help with playground supervision, help with hall duty, help with lunchroom supervision, etc. These types of experiences are a part of education and/or the normal school day and are certainly in order for the student teacher to participate.

8. **How important is the role of the cooperating teacher?**

Perhaps you, more than any other individual, will determine the marketability of the student teacher based on the student teacher evaluation. Naturally, we would like to assume all graduating education majors are competent. However, you play an important role in refining, reinforcing, and shaping these competencies via your modeling and mentoring. The role of the cooperating teacher cannot be overstated.

9. **How can the cooperating teacher help the student teacher improve?**

Giving the student teacher frequent feedback on what she/he is doing is especially important. Giving the feedback in writing and/or formally meeting with the student teacher to discuss their progress is very beneficial. A steno-notebook has been shown to be an effective tool for cooperating teacher/ student teacher communication.

10. **If the student teacher has some definite shortcomings, what does the cooperating teacher do?**

The university coordinator or supervisor should be informed. Specific remedial action can be prescribed to help the student teacher. It is possible that the student teacher may need to be removed from the experience. Specific deficiencies may not have enough time in order to be removed during the experience. In such cases, they are so noted on the final evaluation.

11. **Will having a student teacher allow the cooperating teacher extra time to devote to other endeavors?**

Supervising a student teacher is not easy and it does increase one's overall responsibilities. However, because you are helping to train the student teacher to assume many of your responsibilities, your time will be used differently. Whereas your teaching duties may be lessened, time spent in supervising will be increased.

12. **Can student teachers be used as a substitute teacher if the cooperating teacher is absent from the classroom?**

The answer to this question is *no*. Student teachers are not certified teachers and therefore should not be given such a responsibility. Should the cooperating teacher be absent from the classroom, the student teacher can do most or all of the teaching for the day. However, there needs to be a certified substitute teacher in the room to maintain a sense of liability for the school system.

13. **What do student teachers do when they must be absent from the classroom? How many times may they miss before they are considered unable to fulfill their obligations for student teaching?**

Student teachers may miss school days due to any number of reasons just as a regular classroom teacher. If a student teacher misses more than six days for sickness, personal injury, bereavement, interviews, etc., they may be withdrawn or given an incomplete for the experience. An "NC" will be recorded if the student is withdrawn after the last day to drop without penalty.

The decision to terminate a student teaching assignment due to too many absences from duty is the responsibility of the university coordinator acting in concert with the supervisor, cooperating teacher, building principal, and director of student field experiences. The student teacher, however, may be permitted to make up the days missed by extending the student teaching period, thus making the decision for termination null and void. Consideration should be given to this option instead of termination, provided the performance level of the student teacher indicates potential for completion of the experience with a "competent" or higher evaluation.

Unplanned absences do happen, however. In such cases, the student teacher must notify their cooperating teacher and university coordinator or supervisor by phone before 7:30 a.m. When absence occurs during the time, the student teacher is responsible for all of the teaching—the lesson plans for all presentations must be available and sufficiently detailed so the cooperating teacher or a substitute teacher can teach the curriculum.

A planned absence must be requested a minimum of 48 hours in advance. While requests are usually approved, they may be denied. If previous absences total six or more, planned absences should be of the utmost importance.

14. **What are the advantages of working with student teachers?**

One can hardly call the monetary remuneration for working with a student teacher an advantage. However, there are other significant advantages. First, supervising a student teacher enables one to refine, reinforce, or reshape their own teaching skills due to the fact they are serving as a model. Second, working with a student teacher can act as a self-serving experience for personal growth and a self-renewal experience. Third, many cooperating teachers have expressed a pleasant feeling knowing they have played a significant role in helping to shape a young student teacher who has the potential to be a teacher. In so doing, they are helping to propagate exemplary education.

15. **How will the student teacher be evaluated?**

Evaluation must be a continuous process, and as the student teacher grows, she/he will develop skills of self-evaluation. In the meantime, ongoing evaluation is achieved through daily and weekly conferences with the cooperating teacher, the university coordinator or supervisor, as well as written evaluations.

16. **Are student teachers allowed to work while they are completing their student teaching experience?**

Employment during student teaching is discouraged. Student teaching is considered to be a full-time responsibility. If a student teacher is employed prior to student teaching, he/she is encouraged to discontinue employment. Remember that student teachers are guests in school systems. The students in the classroom(s) deserve undivided attention. The university coordinator has the right to terminate or alter a student teacher's work schedule if he/she believes it is interfering with the student teacher's classroom performance that could result in a less than desirable evaluation.

17. **Are student teachers allowed to coach while completing their student teaching experience?**

Any student teacher wishing to coach must do so as a volunteer. He/she must let the university coordinator know of his/her desire to coach. The university coordinator has the right to terminate or alter a student teacher's coaching experience if he/she believes it is interfering with the student teacher's classroom performance.

# B. Planned Absence Request Form

_____

Name of Student Teacher

Today's date _____ Date(s) of leave _____

_____ _____ a.m. _____ p.m. _____ both

**Reason for absence:**

_____

_____

**Contingency Plan:** _(Specify who will assume your duties and/or where the directions for these duties can be found. If this were unexpected and you were to teach, did you provide substitute lesson plans?)_

_____

_____

_____

Signed. _____
　　　　　　　　　(Student Teacher)

Signed. _____
　　　　　　　　(Cooperating Teacher)

**Cooperating Teacher please check one:**

_____ Approved      _____ Not Approved

# C. Student Teacher PreK-12 Observation Form

**Directions:** During the first week of each experience, complete this observation sheet and share it with your cooperating teacher.

Date _____ Time of Day _____

Situation *(What is happening in class at this time?)* _____

---

1. Which students appear to be leaders?

2. Which students finish their work first? What is the quality of the completed work?

3. Which students finish their work last? What is the quality of the completed work?

4. What do the students do in their free moments?

5. In what way do the students show their interest in or indifference to what is going on?

6. Which students consistently show cooperative behavior?

7. Which students are using a form of technology to enhance their learning?

8. Which students tend to be noisy and disorderly? Under what conditions are these behaviors observed?

9. Which students participate in group activities?

10. Which students do not participate in group activities?

11. Which students seem to demand more than their share of the teacher's time or attention? How do they do this?

# D. Two-Week Progress Report

Student Teacher: _____

**Directions to cooperating teachers**: Please complete, discuss, and sign this form. Have your student teacher send or bring it to his/her coordinator or supervisor at the end of the second week of the student teaching experience.

**The student teacher has had the following experiences in the past two weeks: (Check all that apply.)**

_____ 1.  Observed and discussed observations with the cooperating teacher.

_____ 2.  Learned names of pupils in his or her classroom.

_____ 3.  Has read and discussed school policies and classroom policies.

_____ 4.  Has taken responsibility for some parts of the classroom routines.

_____ 5.  Has aided pupils during supervised study time.

_____ 6.  Has co-planned/co-taught 1–2 lessons.

_____ 7.  Has done some independent teaching in either a small-group or large-group setting.

_____ 8.  Is acquainted with neighbor or department faculty, the administration, and staff.

**Directions to cooperating teachers**: **Circle** the word(s) that best reflect your student teacher's characteristics at this time.

**The student teacher's:**

1.  Enthusiasm is (acceptable    needs improvement.)
2.  Punctuality is (acceptable    needs improvement.)
3.  Academic preparation is (acceptable    needs improvement.)
4.  Knowledge of lesson plans is acceptable or needs improvement.
5.  Rapport and personal relations with pupils are (acceptable    needs improvement.)
6.  Poise in a large group is (acceptable    needs improvement.)
7.  Oral grammar and written communication is (acceptable    needs improvement.)
8.  Cooperation with you and pupils is (acceptable    needs improvement.)
9.  Overall commitment to this assignment is (acceptable    needs improvement.)
10. Knowledge of technology's application for student learning and professional decision making is (acceptable    needs improvement.)
11. Attire is (acceptable    needs improvement.)

**Comments:**

**Signatures** _____    _____
          (Cooperating Teacher)                (Student Teacher)

# E. Student Teaching Schedule Form

**Directions:** Use the space below to indicate your long-range plans for taking on responsibilities during student teaching. Indicate when you will take over classes, when you will teach your unit, and when your cooperating teacher(s) will take back the teaching responsibilities. This planning should be completed with your cooperating teacher. It should be somewhat reflective of the eight-week prescription listed in the book. Share this outline with your university coordinator and/or supervisor once the schedule is completed.

| Week | Monday | Tuesday | Wednesday | Thursday | Friday |
|------|--------|---------|-----------|----------|--------|
| 1 |  |  |  |  |  |
| 2 |  |  |  |  |  |
| 3 |  |  |  |  |  |
| 4 |  |  |  |  |  |
| 5 |  |  |  |  |  |
| 6 |  |  |  |  |  |
| 7 |  |  |  |  |  |
| 8 |  |  |  |  |  |

## F. Weekly Schedule Form

**WEEKLY SCHEDULE FOR STUDENT TEACHING PRACTICUM**

Name _____

School Name _____

School Phone _____

| Period | Time | Room # | Monday | Tuesday | Wednesday | Thursday | Friday | Notes |
|---|---|---|---|---|---|---|---|---|
| 1 | | | | | | | | |
| 2 | | | | | | | | |
| 3 | | | | | | | | |
| 4 | | | | | | | | |
| 5 | | | | | | | | |
| 6 | | | | | | | | |
| 7 | | | | | | | | |
| Extra-Curricular | | | | | | | | |

Arrival Time for Teachers _____

Arrival Time for Pupils _____

Dismissal Time for Pupils _____

Dismissal Time for Teachers _____

Lunch Times _____

Known dates school will not be in session

Dates                    Reason

_____    _____

_____    _____

_____    _____

# G.  Statement of Commitment & Acknowledgement of Consequences

I have read the Student Teaching Pledge found in the UNI Student Teaching Handbook and the Iowa Code of Professional Conduct and Ethics (complete text found at: http://www.boee.iowa.gov/doc/ethHndot.pdf). I believe that adhering to all the tenets in these documents are critical for my success in student teaching. I am committed to growing throughout my student teaching experience and demonstrating excellence in these tenets.

I understand I will transition into the lead teacher in the classroom through a series of gradual steps, from a short period of observation, to providing support to my cooperating teacher by helping individual students, taking small groups of students for instruction, co-planning with my cooperating teacher, team teaching with my cooperating teacher, serving as a lead teacher for a class/subject area, and gradually adding a class/subject area until I am leading classes/subject areas for the entire day.

I understand that my Student Teaching Coordinator(s) and my Cooperating Teacher(s) or other professional colleagues will provide constructive criticism of my performance to help me grow as a teacher. I will respond positiviely to this constructive criticism and use it in my next teaching sequences.

## Acknowledgement of Consequences

I also understand that student teaching is my priority. I understand my cooperating teacher/student teaching coordinator will identify my areas of strength and weaknesses and will help me work on each. I understand if I continue to struggle or do not work on identified areas of weakness, I will receive a Notice of Concern (NOC). I know I should look to the NOC as an opportunity to focus on improvement. In most cases, student teachers focus and demonstrate improvement and the NOC is resolved. Should I not improve, I realize there will be consequences. (More on Professional Competencies and NOC can be found at www.uni.edu/teachered/professional-competencies.)

If at any time I am removed from my student teaching placement, at the request of the school or the student teaching coordinator, or I fail to show adequate ratings on the student teaching final evaluation, I will receive No Credit (NC) for this placement. I understand I will then have to make a written application for the next student teaching placement and will have to complete and pay for an additional eight weeks of student teaching placement. Please be advised, if a student teacher receives No Credit from **two** student teaching placements s/he cannot be recommended for teacher licensure by the University of Northern Iowa. If I withdraw from student teaching, I understand I will receive an NOC documenting my withdrawal and explaining the next steps should I want to obtain my teaching certificate in the future.

_____

UNI Student ID

_____

Printed Name

_____

Date

_____

Signature

**MIDTERM EVALUATION
OF
STUDENT TEACHING**

Name: _____

| Last | First | Middle/Maiden |

Student ID Number        Major

| Grade Level(s) | Building(s) | School District |

| City | State | Zip Code |

| University Coordinator | Clinical Supervisor | Cooperating Teacher |

Office _____ | | Building

Phone   Area | Beginning and Ending Dates | Phone   Area

Evaluation Scale: NA..Not Applicable; ME..Minimal Evidence; B..Beginning; E..Emerging; P..Proficient; A..Advanced      Check the Appropriate Circle

### COMPETENCIES/CHARACTERISTICS      PERFORMANCE LEVELS

| | | NA | ME | B | E | P | A |
|---|---|----|----|---|---|---|---|
| 1. | **Learner Development** <br> Understands how learners grow and develop, recognizing that patterns of learning and development vary individually within and across the cognitive, linguistic, social, emotional, and physical areas; designs and implements developmentally appropriate and challenging learning experiences. | O | O | O | O | O | O |
| 2. | **Learning Differences** <br> Uses understanding of individual differences and diverse cultures and communities to ensure inclusive learning environments that enable each learner to meet high standards. | O | O | O | O | O | O |
| 3. | **Learning Environments** <br> Works with others to create environments that support individual and collaborative learning; encourages positive social interaction, active engagement in learning, and self motivation. | O | O | O | O | O | O |
| 4. | **Content Knowledge** <br> Understands the central concepts, tools of inquiry, and structures of the discipline(s) and creates learning experiences that make the discipline accessible and meaningful for learners to assure mastery of content. | O | O | O | O | O | O |
| 5. | **Application of Content** <br> Understands how to connect concepts and use differing perspectives to engage learners in critical thinking, creativity, and collaborative problem solving related to authentic local and global issues. | O | O | O | O | O | O |
| 6. | **Assessment** <br> Understands and uses multiple methods of assessment to engage learners in their own growth, to monitor learner progress, and to guide teacher's and learner's decision making. | O | O | O | O | O | O |
| 7. | **Planning for Instruction** <br> Plans instruction that supports every student in meeting rigorous learning goals; draws upon knowledge of content areas, curriculum, cross-disciplinary skills, and pedagogy, and knowledge of learners and community context. | O | O | O | O | O | O |
| 8. | **Instructional Strategies** <br> Understands and uses a variety of instructional strategies to encourage learners to develop deep understanding of content and their connections; builds skills to apply knowledge in meaningful ways. | O | O | O | O | O | O |
| 9. | **Professional Learning and Ethical Practice** <br> Engages in ongoing professional learning; uses evidence to continually evaluate own practice; adapts practice to meet needs of each learner. | O | O | O | O | O | O |
| 10. | **Leadership and Collaboration** <br> Seeks appropriate leadership roles and opportunities to take responsibility for student learning; collaborates with learners, families, colleagues, to ensure learner growth and advance the profession. | O | O | O | O | O | O |

**UNI**versity of Northern Iowa
College of Education
Office of Student Field Experiences
Cedar Falls, IA  50614

**FINAL EVALUATION
OF
STUDENT TEACHING**

Name: _____

| Last | First | Middle/Maiden |

_____

Student ID Number             Major

_____

Grade Level(s)          Building(s)          School District

_____

City          State          Zip Code

_____

University Coordinator      Clinical Supervisor      Cooperating Teacher

Office _____        Building _____

Phone    Area          Beginning and Ending Dates      Phone    Area

Evaluation Scale:  NA..Not Applicable; ME..Minimal Evidence;  B..Beginning; E..Emerging; P..Proficient; A..Advanced      Check the Appropriate Circle

| COMPETENCIES/CHARACTERISTICS | NA | ME | B | E | P | A |
|---|---|---|---|---|---|---|
| 1. **Learner Development** Understands how learners grow and develop, recognizing that patterns of learning and development vary individually within and across the cognitive, linguistic, social, emotional, and physical areas; designs and implements developmentally appropriate and challenging learning experiences. | O | O | O | O | O | O |
| 2. **Learning Differences** Uses understanding of individual differences and diverse cultures and communities to ensure inclusive learning environments that enable each learner to meet high standards. | O | O | O | O | O | O |
| 3. **Learning Environments** Works with others to create environments that support individual and collaborative learning; encourages positive social interaction, active engagement in learning, and self motivation. | O | O | O | O | O | O |
| 4. **Content Knowledge** Understands the central concepts, tools of inquiry, and structures of the discipline(s) and creates learning experiences that make the discipline accessible and meaningful for learners to assure mastery of content. | O | O | O | O | O | O |
| 5. **Application of Content** Understands how to connect concepts and use differing perspectives to engage learners in critical thinking, creativity, and collaborative problem solving related to authentic local and global issues. | O | O | O | O | O | O |
| 6. **Assessment** Understands and uses multiple methods of assessment to engage learners in their own growth, to monitor learner progress, and to guide teacher's and learner's decision making. | O | O | O | O | O | O |
| 7. **Planning for Instruction** Plans instruction that supports every student in meeting rigorous learning goals; draws upon knowledge of content areas, curriculum, cross-disciplinary skills, and pedagogy, and knowledge of learners and community context. | O | O | O | O | O | O |
| 8. **Instructional Strategies** Understands and uses a variety of instructional strategies to encourage learners to develop deep understanding of content and their connections; builds skills to apply knowledge in meaningful ways. | O | O | O | O | O | O |
| 9. **Professional Learning and Ethical Practice** Engages in ongoing professional learning; uses evidence to continually evaluate own practice; adapts practice to meet needs of each learner. | O | O | O | O | O | O |
| 10. **Leadership and Collaboration** Seeks appropriate leadership roles and opportunities to take responsibility for student learning; collaborates with learners, families, colleagues, to ensure learner growth and advance the profession. | O | O | O | O | O | O |

UNIversity of Northern Iowa
College of Education
Office of Student Field Experiences
Cedar Falls, IA 50614

**MIDTERM EVALUATION**
**OF**
**EARLY CHILDHOOD STUDENT TEACHING**

Name: _____

| Last | First | Middle/Maiden |

Student ID Number                                      Major

Grade Level(s)                    Building(s)                    School District

City                              State                          Zip Code

University Coordinator            Clinical Supervisor            Cooperating Teacher

Office _____                                          Building
Phone    Area                  Beginning and Ending Dates        Phone    Area

Evaluation Scale: U...Unsatisfactory; CO...Competent; HC...Highly Competent; O...Outstanding                Check the Appropriate Circle

| COMPETENCIES/CHARACTERISTICS | PERFORMANCE LEVELS | | | | |
| --- | --- | --- | --- | --- | --- |
| | U | LC | CO | HC | O |
| 1. **Knowledge of Care-Giving and Skills Areas** Understands the central concepts of nurturing and care-giving; understands ages and stages of early childhood; plans and prepares nutritious foods when appropriate. | O | O | O | O | O |
| 2. **Knowledge of Learners and Learning Process** Understands how children learn and differ in their approaches to learning; provides learning opportunities and experiences that are meaningful and that support their development cognitively, socially, emotionally, physically and culturally; understands learners as a group and as individuals. | O | O | O | O | O |
| 3. **Instructional Planning** Plans instruction with children's health and safety as priority; understands, develops and implements curriculum based on knowledge of subject matter, students' interests, developmental levels, the community, state/district/accreditation standards, and curriculum goals. | O | O | O | O | O |
| 4. **Use of Instructional Strategies** Understands and uses a variety of instructional strategies; adapts teaching, curriculum, and care-giving styles to the diverse needs of students; understands and uses an appropriate balance between indirect and direct instruction; recognizes and capitalizes on teachable moments. | O | O | O | O | O |
| 5. **Learning Environment** Creates a safe and healthy learning environment that encourages positive social interaction, active engagement in learning and self-motivation; fosters independence through accessible materials and toys; demonstrates a positive, enthusiastic attitude toward learners and the task of teaching; able to recognize unsafe situations and act upon them in a timely fashion. | O | O | O | O | O |
| 6. **Classroom Management** Creates a fair, respectful, positive environment; sets clear expectations and reasonable consequences; uses both direct and indirect guidance techniques to encourage appropriate positive personal behavior choices; honors children's choices when appropriate; able to treat each child with dignity and as an individual. | O | O | O | O | O |
| 7. **Use of Communication Strategies** Uses knowledge of both oral, and non-verbal communication techniques to foster active inquiry, collaboration and supportive interactions that are developmentally appropriate. | O | O | O | O | O |
| 8. **Use of Assessing/Diagnosing/Evaluating Strategies** Understands and uses a variety of formal, informal, and authentic assessment strategies that align with instructional approaches; takes actions to determine what strengths and problems exist and responds appropriately to the assessment results; evaluates in an objective manner. | O | O | O | O | O |
| 9. **Use of Motivational Strategies** Uses multiple techniques, materials, and settings to kindle and sustain interest of learners; motivates by personal behavior; able to identify interest and non-interest behaviors and respects them. | O | O | O | O | O |
| 10. **Use of Problem-Solving/Decision Making Strategies** Reflects on teaching during and after lessons in order to recognize and solve problems and make decisions; examines situations from various perspectives and is appropriately decisive; able to seek out information from others and other sources to solve instructional or behavioral problems. | O | O | O | O | O |
| 11. **Home-School-Community Relations** Fosters relationships with colleagues, parents, and, as needed, agencies in the larger community. | O | O | O | O | O |
| 12. **Use of Technology** Integrates the computer and other high- and low-technology into preparation, classroom teaching activites, assessment and/or documentation. | O | O | O | O | O |
| 13. **Use of Multicultural Gender Fair (MCGF) Strategies** Demonstrates sensitivity to family, community diversity and cultural identity; infuses MCGF strategies into all professional interactions. | O | O | O | O | O |
| 14. **Human Relations Skills** Implements sound human relations and communication skills in order to foster productive, positive learning communities. | O | O | O | O | O |
| 15. **Professional Characteristics and Leadership** Exhibits high quality characteristics in professional and personal demeanor; professional behavior exemplifies role awareness and ethical conduct; takes initiative, recognizes and functions in the role of leader, or as an integral part of the staff, and takes on the appropriate role at the required time. | O | O | O | O | O |

UNIversity of Northern Iowa
College of Education
Office of Student Field Experiences
Cedar Falls, IA 50614

**FINAL EVALUATION**
**OF**
**EARLY CHILDHOOD  STUDENT TEACHING**

Name: _____
         Last                                      First                                      Middle/Maiden

_____
         Student ID Number                                      Major

_____
         Grade Level(s)                        Building(s)                        School District

_____
         City                                      State                                      Zip Code

_____
         University Coordinator              Clinical Supervisor              Cooperating Teacher

Office _____      _____      Building
Phone      Area                      Beginning and Ending Dates      Phone      Area _____

Evaluation Scale:  U...Unsatisfactory;  CO...Competent;  HC...Highly Competent;  O...Outstanding          Check the Appropriate Circle

| COMPETENCIES/CHARACTERISTICS | U | LC | CO | HC | O |
|---|---|---|---|---|---|
| 1. **Knowledge of Care-Giving and Skills Areas** <br> Understands the central concepts of nurturing and care-giving; understands ages and stages of early childhood; plans and prepares nutritious foods when appropriate. | O | O | O | O | O |
| 2. **Knowledge of Learners and Learning Process** <br> Understands how children learn and differ in their approaches to learning; provides learning opportunities and experiences that are meaningful and that support their development cognitively, socially, emotionally, physically and culturally; understands learners as a group and as individuals. | O | O | O | O | O |
| 3. **Instructional Planning** <br> Plans instruction with children's health and safety as priority; understands, develops and implements curriculum based on knowledge of subject matter, students' interests, developmental levels, the community, state/district/accreditation standards, and curriculum goals. | O | O | O | O | O |
| 4. **Use of Instructional Strategies** <br> Understands and uses a variety of instructional strategies; adapts teaching, curriculum, and care-giving styles to the diverse needs of students; understands and uses an appropriate balance between indirect and direct instruction; recognizes and capitalizes on teachable moments. | O | O | O | O | O |
| 5. **Learning Environment** <br> Creates a safe and healthy learning environment that encourages positive social interaction, active engagement in learning and self-motivation; fosters independence through accessible materials and toys; demonstrates a positive, enthusiastic attitude toward learners and the task of teaching; able to recognize unsafe situations and act upon them in a timely fashion. | O | O | O | O | O |
| 6. **Classroom Management** <br> Creates a fair, respectful, positive environment; sets clear expectations and reasonable consequences; uses both direct and indirect guidance techniques to encourage appropriate positive personal behavior choices; honors children's choices when appropriate; able to treat each child with dignity and as an individual. | O | O | O | O | O |
| 7. **Use of Communication Strategies** <br> Uses knowledge of both oral, and non-verbal communication techniques to foster active inquiry, collaboration and supportive interactions that are developmentally appropriate. | O | O | O | O | O |
| 8. **Use of Assessing/Diagnosing/Evaluating Strategies** <br> Understands and uses a variety of formal, informal, and authentic assessment strategies that align with instructional approaches; takes actions to determine what strengths and problems exist and responds appropriately to the assessment results; evaluates in an objective manner. | O | O | O | O | O |
| 9. **Use of Motivational Strategies** <br> Uses multiple techniques, materials, and settings to kindle and sustain interest of learners; motivates by personal behavior; able to identify interest and non-interest behaviors and respects them. | O | O | O | O | O |
| 10. **Use of Problem-Solving/Decision Making Strategies** <br> Reflects on teaching during and after lessons in order to recognize and solve problems and make decisions; examines situations from various perspectives and is appropriately decisive; able to seek out information from others and other sources to solve instructional or behavioral problems. | O | O | O | O | O |
| 11. **Home-School-Community Relations** <br> Fosters relationships with colleagues, parents, and, as needed, agencies in the larger community. | O | O | O | O | O |
| 12. **Use of Technology** <br> Integrates the computer and other high- and low-technology into preparation, classroom teaching activites, assessment and/or documentation. | O | O | O | O | O |
| 13. **Use of Multicultural Gender Fair (MCGF) Strategies** <br> Demonstrates sensitivity to family, community diversity and cultural identity; infuses MCGF strategies into all professional interactions. | O | O | O | O | O |
| 14. **Human Relations Skills** <br> Implements sound human relations and communication skills in order to foster productive, positive learning communities. | O | O | O | O | O |
| 15. **Professional Characteristics and Leadership** <br> Exhibits high quality characteristics in professional and personal demeanor; professional behavior exemplifies role awareness and ethical conduct; takes initiative, recognizes and functions in the role of leader, or as an integral part of the staff, and takes on the appropriate role at the required time. | O | O | O | O | O |

# University of Northern Iowa Teacher Candidate Dispositions

This form will be used to evaluate the professionalism displayed by a student teacher. It will be used to document professional progress in the areas of Collaboration, Honesty and Integrity, Respect, Commitment to Learning, Emotional Maturity, Leadership and Responsibility. Dispositions are behaviors that constitute the habits of one's lifestyle and are often referred to as "temperaments." Teacher candidates are expected to exhibit desirable dispositions that enhance student learning.

| Student Teacher Name | Cooperating Teacher Name | Date | Semester | UNI Coordinator |
|---|---|---|---|---|
|  |  |  |  |  |

| Not Applicable | Concerns | Needs Improvement | Emerging | Acceptable |
|---|---|---|---|---|
| NA | 0 | 1 | 2 | 3 |
| Does not apply of there has been limited opportunity to demonstrate the desired behavior | The student displays behaviors contrary to those expected for this disposition. | The student teacher rarely displays the desired behaviors. | The student is at an emergent level; the behaviors might not be consistent. | The student consistently displays the desired behaviors deemed appropriate for student teaching. |

| **Collaboration**: Teacher collaborates with learners, colleagues, school leaders, families, members of the learners' communities, and community organizations to better understand students and maximize their learning. |  |  |  |  |  |
|---|---|---|---|---|---|
| 1.1 Interacts constructively with peers/colleagues, administrators, supervisors, staff, and cooperating teachers <ul><li>Shows consideration and respect for the thoughts and feelings of others</li><li>Demonstrates effective verbal and non-verbal communication skills</li><li>Demonstrates flexibility with others</li><li>Solicits suggestions and feedback from others</li><li>Listens and responds to others</li><li>Maintains communication with colleagues, supervisors, and mentor teachers when questions or concerns arise</li><li>Recognizes a range of valid viewpoints</li></ul> | NA | 0 | 1 | 2 | 3 |
| 1.2 Functions as a contributing member of an instructional team to achieve long-term curriculum goals, state content standards, and district standards <ul><li>Communicates effectively both verbally and non-verbally</li><li>Shares ideas and materials</li><li>Fosters communication among all members of the learning community</li><li>Shows initiative and asks questions about teaching strategies</li></ul> | NA | 0 | 1 | 2 | 3 |
| 1.3 Anticipates instruction needed, allowing for individual differences. Creates learning experiences that accommodate diverse learners. <ul><li>Interaction with family & the broader community are respectful, purposeful, & professional</li><li>Acts as an advocate for learners & partners w/ parents & guardians to provide education</li><li>Promotes cross-curricular understanding</li><li>Knows when and how to access specialized services to meet student needs</li><li>Values diverse languages and dialects</li><li>Values knowledge outside of his/her content area</li></ul> | NA | 0 | 1 | 2 | 3 |
| Comments: |  |  |  |  |  |

| Honesty and Integrity: The student demonstrates truthfulness, professional behavior, and trustworthiness. | | | | | |
|---|---|---|---|---|---|
| 2.1 Displays honesty and integrity<br>• Maintains confidentiality<br>• Elicits trust and respect from both peers and supervisors<br>• Produces original work and credits sources when appropriate<br>2.2 Demonstrates professional relationships<br>• Maintains appropriate relations with students<br>• Demonstrates fairness and respect to all students, colleagues, administrators, and parents | NA | 0 | 1 | 2 | 3 |
| Comments: | | | | | |

| Respect: The student honors, values, and demonstrates consideration and regard for oneself and others. | | | | | |
|---|---|---|---|---|---|
| 3.1 Is respectful of cultural patterns and expectations within a community context<br>• Presents self in a professional manner (e.g., dress, communication)<br>• Speaks and behaves in a manner that is sensitive to linguistic and cultural differences and respects the dignity and worth of others<br>• Establishes good rapport with students and colleagues<br>• Seeks to address the varied learning needs of students in his/her classroom, especially for learners with disabilities and language learning needs<br>• Practices patience and empathy | NA | 0 | 1 | 2 | 3 |
| Comments: | | | | | |

| Professionalism and continued growth: The student values learning for self and students. Models behaviors that positively impact student learning. | | | | | |
|---|---|---|---|---|---|
| 4.1 Exhibits energy, drive, and determination to make one's school and classroom the best possible environment for teaching and learning<br>• Plans and delivers instruction that engages all students in his/her classroom and addresses their learning needs<br>• Values ongoing assessment as essential to the instructional process<br>• Believes that plans must always be open to adjustment and revision | NA | 0 | 1 | 2 | 3 |
| 4.2 Demonstrates a commitment to students' learning<br>• Implements research-based strategies<br>• Proposes ideas and solutions that address curriculum, instruction, and classroom management<br>• Locates and/or creates materials that engage student learning<br>• Assumes responsibilities, locates materials and resources, and improves teaching<br>• Reflects upon and evaluates effectiveness as a teacher, and seeks to improve skills<br>• Reflects on and offers ideas to address curricular, instructional ,and classroom management matters<br>• Engages students in discovering how knowledge is constructed<br>• Actively and consciously looks for stories, wisdom, action, and creations of knowledge from diverse perspectives | NA | 0 | 1 | 2 | 3 |

| 4.3 Reflects on performance and attitudes as a teacher | NA | 0 | 1 | 2 | 3 |
|---|---|---|---|---|---|
| • Reflects upon and evaluates effectiveness as a teacher, and seeks to improve skills<br>• Receives feedback in a positive manner and makes necessary adjustments<br>• Regularly re-assesses his/her commitment to the profession<br>• Evaluates instruction and student interactions and modifies instruction as needed<br>• Expresses a passion for teaching and learning<br>• Performs work that reflects best effort | | | | | |

Comments:

---

**Emotional Maturity**: The student demonstrates appropriate behavior.

| 5.1 Demonstrates self-confidence and enthusiasm | NA | 0 | 1 | 2 | 3 |
|---|---|---|---|---|---|
| • Displays enthusiasm for teaching and the subject matter<br>• Demonstrates self-confidence through body language, voice tone, eye contact, preparedness<br>• Exhibits energy, drive, and determination to become a professional educator<br>• Is a positive person who can exhibit the joy of teaching | | | | | |
| 5.2 Understands he/she must be dependable, conscientious, and punctual | NA | 0 | 1 | 2 | 3 |
| • Arrives early or on-time<br>• Completes assigned tasks in a timely manner<br>• Follows through with assignments and expectations | | | | | |
| 5.3 Models the social skills, character traits, and dispositions desired in students | NA | 0 | 1 | 2 | 3 |
| • Establishes caring and mutually respectful relationships with students<br>• Explicitly teaches and models desired behaviors and attitudes | | | | | |

Comments:

---

**Leadership and Responsibility**: The student acts independently and demonstrates accountability, reliability, and sound judgment.

| 6.1 Understands the expectation of the profession including codes of ethics, professional standards of practice, and relevant law and policy | NA | 0 | 1 | 2 | 3 |
|---|---|---|---|---|---|
| • Has obtained and read school policy manual<br>• Adheres to class, school, and district rules and policies | | | | | |
| 6.2 Advises students in formal and informal settings | NA | 0 | 1 | 2 | 3 |
| • Shows concern for all aspects of a student's well-being, is alert to signs of academic and behavioral difficulty, and responds appropriately<br>• Actively listens to and advises students, making referrals as appropriate | | | | | |
| 6.3 Meets work schedule demands | NA | 0 | 1 | 2 | 3 |
| • Prepares lessons and demonstrations other responsibilities<br>• Meets and consults with cooperating teacher each week to plan lessons<br>• Demonstrates punctuality and is present for additional activities in addition to regular teaching schedule | | | | | |

| | NA | 0 | 1 | 2 | 3 |
|---|---|---|---|---|---|
| 6.4 Awareness of the importance of professional appearance and demeanor<br>  • Dresses professionally<br>  • Displays a positive attitude<br>  • Communicates in a professional manner<br>  • Accepts responsibility for own actions | NA | 0 | 1 | 2 | 3 |
| 6.5 Demonstrates initiative, in an acceptable manner, for introducing programs or practices in a school or classroom<br>  • Makes suggestions to cooperating teacher or at faculty meetings<br>  • Offers ideas to mentor teacher and other instructional team members around instructional, curricular, and behavioral needs of students | NA | 0 | 1 | 2 | 3 |
| Comments: | | | | | |

*\*\*\*This is the "Iowa Dispositions Model: A Framework for Developing Effective Teacher Dispositions" which was developed as a part of the Iowa Teacher Quality Enhancement Grant. Revised by Lori A. Smith, UNI—Fall 2013*

**Signature of the Student Who Has Read This Form:**


_____

Signature of Student                                    Signature of Cooperating Teacher


_____

Signature of UNI Coordinator                        Date

# Letter for Reapplication for Student Teaching

To: Student teachers whom have received a **Withdrawal (W)** and/or a **No Credit (NC)** in a student teaching placement

RE : Reapplication Procedure to request an additional student teaching placement

According to the procedures in the UNI Student Teaching Handbook, since you were not successful in one of your previous student teaching placements and you wish to have another student teaching placement you will need to write a formal letter to the Teacher Education Council.  In this letter you need to:

- Introduce yourself

- Explain why your previous student teaching experience was unsuccessful. (Be specific identifying the specific aspects of teaching you were unable to demonstrate.)

- Identify what type of placement (content area and grade span) you need, how long a placement you are requesting, and during what semester/year you hope to be placed, and where you would hope to be placed.  (It is the general policy that you will be placed in a new center with a new student teaching coordinator.)

- Provide reasons why you feel you should be allowed another student teaching placement.

- Explain what has changed in your abilities and/or effort that would indicate you would be successful in a new student teaching placement.

- Provide any documentation that supports your request.

- Address your letter to Teacher Education Council and email it to the following coordinators:

    - Coordinator of Elementary Teacher Education

    - Coordinator of Secondary Teacher Education

    - Coordinator of Student Teaching

There are several important aspects of this process:  when you were not successful in a student teaching placement this is one strike.  If you are not successful in a second student teaching placement (8 wk), that will constitute two strikes.  Student with two strikes will not be recommended for licensure by UNI. If you have enough credits you could graduate with a B.A. without teacher licensure.  If the Coordinators of Teacher Education recommend placement, you will be placed in a different center from your prior unsuccessful student teaching placement. The Coordinator of Student Teaching will work with the Student Teaching Coordinators to obtain a placement for the semester requested.  Realize if the timeline is short, a placement may not be possible for the semester requested, but we will make every effort to obtain a student teaching placement during the next closest semester.  Students will have to pay for additional student teaching placement credit hours and all associated fees.

# Important URLs

The following URLs are important to this handbook. Reference to specific URLs can also be found in the text of the handbook.

General listing for the College of Education
http://www.uni.edu/coe

General listing for student teaching
http://www.uni.edu/coe/departments/student-teaching

General listing for teacher education
http://www.uni.edu/teached/

University policy relating to personal conduct
http://www.uni.edu/policies/303

UNI Career Center
http://www.uni.edu/careerservices/

Board of Educational Examiners for Iowa
http://www.boee.iowa.gov/

Teach Iowa
http://www.teachiowa.gov/

Iowa Regional Education Applicant Placement Program
http://www.iareap.net

Midterm & Final Evaluation Forms
http://www.uni.edu/coe/departments/office-student-field-experiences/information-faculty/supervisors